PERSPECTIVES

A Multicultural Portrait of

World War II

By David K. Wright

Marshall Cavendish
New York • London • Toronto

Cover: April 1943: Japanese-American troops enthusiastically face the camera upon arrival at their new training center in Mississippi. Like most U.S. troops grouped in fighting units according to racial or ethnic background, these soldiers are led by a white officer. Many loyal Americans distinguished themselves in battle but remained segregated from troops of white, European-American descent until the Korean War in the 1950s.

Published by
Marshall Cavendish Corporation
2415 Jerusalem Avenue
P.O. Box 587
North Bellmore, New York 11710, USA

© Marshall Cavendish Corporation, 1994

Edited, designed, and produced by Water Buffalo Books, Milwaukee

Project director: Mark Sachner
Art director: Sabine Beaupré
Picture researcher: Diane Laska
Editorial: Valerie Weber
Marshall Cavendish development editor: MaryLee Knowlton
Marshall Cavendish editorial director: Evelyn Fazio

Editorial consultant: Mark S. Guardalabene, Milwaukee Public Schools

Picture Credits: © The Bettmann Archive: Cover, 6, 10, 12, 13, 14, 16, 19, 20 (all), 21 (both), 22, 24, 25, 26 (both), 28-29, 30 (both), 32 (both), 33, 34, 35, 36, 38, 39, 40, 42, 43 (both), 44 (both), 45 (top), 46 (top), 47, 49 (both), 50 (both), 51 (both), 54, 56 (both), 57 (both), 60 (both), 61 (both), 62 (all), 63, 66, 67, 68, 71, 72, 73, 74 (both), 75 (top); © Culver Pictures, Inc.: 8, 11 (both), 23, 27, 45 (bottom), 53, 59; © Charles Phelps Cushing/H. Armstrong Roberts: 31, 52 (bottom); © Reuters/Bettmann Archive: 75 (bottom); © H. Armstrong Roberts: 46 (bottom), 52 (top), 64

Library of Congress Cataloging-in-Publication Data

Wright, David K.
    A multicultural portrait of World War II / [David K. Wright].
        p.   cm. — (Perspectives)
    Includes bibliographical references and index.
    ISBN 1-85435-663-1 :
    1. World War. 1939-1945—Juvenile literature. 2. World War. 1939-1945—Women—Juvenile literature. 3. Minorities—Juvenile literature. [1. World War, 1939-1945. 2. Minorities—History.] I. Title. II. Series: Perspectives (Marshall Cavendish Corporation)
D743.7.W69   1994
940.53—dc20   93-46318
                                                                                                        CIP
                                                                                                        AC

To PS – MS

Printed and bound in the U.S.A.

CONTENTS

About *Perspectives*

Perspectives is a series of multicultural portraits of events and topics in U.S. history. Each book examines events not only from the perspective of the white European-Americans who make up most of the population, but from that of people of color and other ethnic minorities, such as American Indians, African-Americans, Asian-Americans, and Hispanic-Americans. These people, along with women, have been given little attention in traditional accounts of U.S. history. And yet their impact on history has been great.

The terms *American Indian, Hispanic-American, Anglo-American, Black, African-American,* and *Asian-American,* like *European-American* and *white,* are used by the authors in this series to identify people of various national origins. Labeling people is a serious business, and what we call a group depends on many things. For example, a few decades ago it was considered acceptable to use the words *colored* or *Negro* to label people of African origin. Today, these words are outdated and often a sign of ignorance or outright prejudice. Some people even consider *Black* less acceptable than *African-American* because it focuses on a person's skin color rather than national origins. And yet *Black* has many practical uses, particularly to describe people whose origins are not only African but Caribbean or Latin American as well.

If we must label people, it's better to be as specific as possible. That is a goal of *Perspectives* — to be precise and fair in the labeling of people by race, ethnicity, national origin, or other factors, such as gender, sexual orientation, or disability. When necessary and possible, Americans of Mexican origin will be called *Mexican-Americans.* Americans of Irish origin will be called *Irish-Americans,* and so on. The same goes for American Indians: when possible, specific Indians are identified by their tribal names, such as the *Chippewa* or *Mohawk.* But in a discussion of various Indian groups, tribal origins may not always be entirely clear, and so it may be more practical to use *American Indian,* a term that has widespread use among Indians and non-Indians alike.

Even within a group, people may disagree over the labels they prefer for their group: *Black* or *African-American? Hispanic* or *Latino? American Indian* or *Native American? White, Anglo,* or *European-American?* Different situations may call for different labels. The labels used in this book represent an effort to be fair, accurate, and perhaps most importantly, to be mindful of what people choose to call *themselves*.

A Note About *World War II*

The U.S. was a very different place before World War II. Few Americans thought in global terms, and the country paid little attention to such domestic problems as racial injustice. Much of that had changed by war's end, when the U.S. found itself a world leader, and minorities were aware that their treatment had barely improved in hundreds of years; they had been segregated, ignored, belittled, or made victims of open bigotry. Not permitted to compete for higher rank or better pay or skills, women, Blacks, Latinos, and others nevertheless became more visible by their presence on ships, driving supply trucks, on chow lines, on assembly lines, and wherever war was waged.

World War II isn't just about the involvement of U.S. ethnic groups, however. Other people, places, and events had a huge impact on the course of the war. Battles raged in Asia and Africa for more than four years and in Europe for more than two when Japanese planes bombed Pearl Harbor, Hawaii, on December 7, 1941, propelling the United States into war. It is important to know that other people suffered, lost, and gave up more than the average American. Obviously, those Americans who were among the 292,131 U.S. battle deaths sacrificed everything they had.

WWII gave rise to events or movements with enormous consequences for people of various races and ethnic groups. These events include the following:

• The conscientious, planned attempt to wipe out entire races and ethnic and religious groups from the face of the earth. Jews, Gypsies, Slavs, and dissenters were massacred by the millions. From such deliberate planning and execution comes the eerily modern word *genocide*.

• The feeling, especially by African-Americans, that democracy could not be fought for in Europe without being practiced at home. Blacks in postwar years were more dissatisfied than ever with inadequate housing, education, voting rights, jobs, and other facets of daily life. This impatience helped the civil rights movement of the 1960s get off the ground, aimed at creating a more nearly equal society for all minorities.

• The huge loss of life by civilians of many races and nationalities. In addition to military people, more innocent bystanders died in WWII than in any other war, in part because air power and other weapons of mass destruction were used, resulting in deaths at a rate of a million a month for months on end.

• The fact that WWII was more nearly a world war than any other since. Every continent except Antarctica saw conflict on land or in nearby coastal waters. War was all too real to ethnic groups from the southern tip of Alaska's Aleutian Islands to Africa, Siberia, Australia, and many points between.

• The knowledge after August 6, 1945, when an atomic bomb was dropped on Hiroshima, Japan, that no one on earth could go to bed at night completely assured of waking up. The bomb created questions of enormous complexity on when and whether it should be used. In any event, the U.S. emerged from World War II as the world's most powerful nation, and part of that power was derived from atomic weapons, which continue to affect our lives today.

Adolf Hitler as a soldier in the Austrian army during World War I. Hitler believed
Germany's internal enemies had forced the country to seek a humiliating peace in 1918.

CHAPTER ONE

Why Did World War II Begin?

Night fell and the shelling erupted once again. It started with the faraway booms of big guns, followed by the hisses and screams of shells splitting the air. The small German Army private with the large mustache clawed deeper into a muddy trench in World War I France to avoid being wounded or killed. A shell burst nearby, wounding several comrades.

The private and hundreds of thousands of Germans and Austrians on one side, and British, French, Americans, and Italians on the other, were in the same place in September of 1918 as they had been six months earlier. During this stalemate, both sides chopped up areas of Belgium and northern France with tanks and artillery, poisoning the air with gas and raking each other with machine-gun fire. The soldier with the mustache wanted the war to end, but when World War I ceased, he felt cheated. This Austrian native — who believed the armistice of November 11, 1918, meant Germany had been "stabbed in the back" — was Adolf Hitler.

Hitler would never forget that his apparently strong, adopted country had suddenly surrendered. A decorated veteran, he became convinced that enemies within Germany were responsible. Communists, democrats, republicans, pacifists, socialists, foreigners, Jews — Hitler blamed them all for a weak postwar Germany that suffered through a terrible economy in the 1920s and early 1930s. While there were many causes of World War II, Hitler's narrow-minded and unforgiving determination to improve, enlarge, and purify Germany certainly was an important one.

Hardships in the 1920s

For a German nationalist — a person who loved the idea of a strong German state — the years following World War I were difficult. There was little or no work, inflation caused prices to rise almost every day, several industrialized areas had been handed to neighboring countries by the Allies, and, despite the war's losses, the nation seemed crowded. Added to these hardships were increasing numbers of foreigners moving in, out, and around the country, willing to work for less money than the average German and therefore putting natives out of work.

Benito Mussolini salutes as he and Hitler review troops during a visit to Germany by the Italian dictator. Like Hitler, Mussolini fought in World War I. And, like Hitler, he quickly suspended civil liberties after coming to power.

Depending on how they viewed things, German citizens were entranced, skeptical, or upset by new systems of government and ideologies. The most frightening to many middle-class Germans was communism, which favored common ownership of everything from farms to factories, with everyone sharing equally in the harvest or production. Communists had successfully overthrown an old government in nearby Russia in 1917, and governments throughout Europe, especially rickety monarchies, became nervous as communists and socialists gained popularity.

Hitler looked at the map of Europe and smoldered with resentment. The future dictator believed crowded Germans needed "living room" to grow, even if it meant moving out Jews, Slavs, Gypsies, and others he believed to be racially inferior non-Aryan people. The former army private and failed artist endured poverty and a brief prison sentence before being appointed Germany's chancellor in 1933 by the old World War I general, Paul von Hindenberg. In fifteen years, Hitler had moved from the mud of France to the number one office in Germany. He immediately began to violate the Treaty of Versailles, signed at the end of World War I, by recruiting soldiers and building weapons.

The nondescript leader reduced the size of his mustache and enlarged his ambitions. He watched the antics of Italy's dictator, Benito Mussolini, and decided that forceful speeches, torch-lit rallies, and dramatic uniforms would result in more and more Germans waving the flag with the swastika he had personally chosen as the symbol of his political philosophy. Hitler wanted to reach — or return to — a German military state full of mysticism, where everything from the architecture to the complexion of the children somehow proved that Germans were a master race.

The new head of state called his ideas National Socialism (abbreviated as *Nazi*) and his administration the Third Reich, or third empire. Before the second empire, which existed during the administration of a leader named Otto von Bismarck, Germany had been a bunch of small states, sharing little but a common language. Bismarck, who was brilliant at foreign affairs, created a united country in 1871. The original Germany, according to Hitler, was the Holy Roman Empire. It existed from A.D. 962 to 1806 and was led by a long line of Germanic kings, including Charlemagne. The dictator used this historic thread to justify his actions.

Silencing the Opposition

Once he was in power, Hitler encouraged the Reichstag (Germany's parliament) to pass the Enabling Act. This law allowed the chancellor to run the country without consulting a cabinet or the Reichstag itself. The law passed

Benito Mussolini, 1883-1945: the first Fascist

Mussolini was the first modern-day dictator. Adolf Hitler copied many of the Italian's theatrics, from snazzy uniforms and flapping flags to dramatic speeches and the use of violence against people who were weak or held opposing views.

Mussolini was born in a mountain village and fought for Italy alongside the French and English in World War I. Immediately afterward, he founded the Fascist Party, a bunch of toughs who threatened politicians, intimidated the timid Italian government, and seemed to goose step wherever they went. After being named prime minister in 1922, he immediately increased Italy's defense budget, while ignoring the needs of Italy's southern poor. Like Hitler, who seduced many Germans with his vision of a powerful, militaristic German state, Mussolini cultivated an image of Italy as a grand, imperial state reminiscent of ancient Rome. He looked around for enemies in the mid-1930s and, like the Nazis, isolated Jews and other groups from his grand vision. As Mussolini and his vision gained in popularity, many Italians turned against friends and neighbors with whom they had lived peacefully for years. In his search for enemies, Mussolini also found two nations all but unable to fight back — Albania in the Balkan area of Europe and Ethiopia in Africa. People living in these two economically and militarily weaker lands became target practice for the dictator's forces.

But up against the Allies in Africa a few years later, the Italian army began to suffer defeats. Il Duce ("The Leader") lost support at home and had to go into hiding after Italy's surrender in 1943. Hitler was unable to prop up Mussolini, who was shot to death in 1945 by his countrymen and left to dangle upside down beside his girlfriend outside a gasoline station in northern Italy. A sobbing Italian woman approached the scene, pulled a pistol and pumped five bullets into Il Duce's body. "That is for each of my five lost sons," she said, showing how most Italians felt by war's end.

A spellbinding speaker and a wonderful writer who could as easily have been a positive force for Italy, Benito Mussolini is important because he proved that countries other than Germany could fall under the spell of a ranting, bigoted tyrant.

because Hitler arrested the Reichstag's eighty-one communist members and bribed several others, leaving a majority that would pass any laws he wanted them to pass. Shortly afterward, Jews were barred from civil service, all labor unions were suppressed, loyal Nazis were given police and military units to run, and opposition political parties were banned. In effect, a bunch of thugs took over the entire country.

Hitler's first physical attack on a minority group took place on June 30, 1934. Ernst Roehm was a homosexual and a German fascist — a right-wing extremist — who headed a group known as the SA (short for *Sturmabteilung*, or storm troopers, also called Brownshirts). Several of Hitler's friends hated Roehm and his followers. Late one night, Roehm, other SA members who happened to be homosexual, and fellow extremists were rounded up and executed without a trial. They were shot or hanged, not for their sexual orientation, but because they were rival Nazis and their Brownshirts were hard to control. They had been more loyal to Roehm than to Hitler and his henchmen.

With consequences that would be tragic for all of Europe, the Nazis also began planning ways to "purify" Germany by getting rid of its Jewish minority and doing away with people in mental asylums and institutions. Jews were at first excluded from the arts and from several professions, such as medicine or teaching. When ordered to register at the local Nazi headquarters, Jewish citizens complied, thereby furnishing the fascists with a handy list of the Jewish population in every town and village. Nazis might emerge from a beer

Smeared with paint, a Berlin department store owned by German Jews shows the work of Hitler's Nazi supporters in 1938. The six-pointed Star of David and other graffiti warn citizens not to shop at the store. Jews all over Germany were forced out of ownership and most professions throughout the 1930s.

hall or a political meeting and, traveling the streets in a gang, know exactly where to go to smash Jewish shop windows with bricks and beat up Jewish neighbors.

Laws were passed as early as 1935 preventing Jews from marrying non-Jews and depriving them of most other civil rights. Catholics and Protestants who refused to conform to Nazi-sponsored German Christian movements were harassed, but this hazing did not approach in intensity the crusade against the country's 8.3 million Jews. On the evening of November 9, 1938, members of the SS, another military group of storm troopers, smashed and burned so many Jewish storefronts all across the country that the date became known as *Kristallnacht,* "the night of broken glass."

Jews who attempted to leave Germany found discrimination in other countries. The United States, for example, welcomed artists, composers, writers, and such luminaries as scientist Albert Einstein but turned away middle-class and blue-collar Jews whose only crime was that they had led quiet lives before the rise of Hitler. In fact, the only place that consistently

Germans, Jews, and Nazi vengeance

Citizens of the U.S. who wondered how European Jews felt about Hitler did not have to look far in late 1938. On November 7, a teenage Polish Jew named Herschel Grynszpan drew a pistol in Paris and shot to death a minor official in the German embassy. Grynszpan told French authorities he killed the German in revenge for Nazi mistreatment of fellow Jews.

Hitler learned immediately of the incident and is said to have thrown a tantrum. He ordered the Nazi propaganda machine to encourage the worst pogrom (organized persecution) of Jews in modern-day Germany. All Jews, Hitler told his countrymen, were to be punished, even though they did not even share the same citizenship as the young gunman.

German non-Jews responded with frightening enthusiasm. Within a few days of Grynszpan's confession, a grisly wave of vandalism swept the Third Reich.

Some 35 Jews were killed, hundreds injured, thousands arrested without cause and heavily fined, 7,500 shops vandalized, and 119 synagogues wrecked, their religious books, scrolls, and artifacts strewn in town and city streets. Broken glass was so plentiful that the November 9 vandalism became known as *Kristallnacht,* night of broken glass.

Kristallnacht should be remembered because it shows one terrifying method the Nazis used to keep order. If an enemy harmed a Nazi, the Nazis killed dozens of the enemy's family, friends, fellow communists, members of that enemy's religion, and so on. This method was repeated throughout the war. For example, when Czech partisans assassinated Reinhard Heydrich, chief of Germany's Security Police, midway through the war, German troops in turn executed a reported 1,331 Czechs.

welcomed Jews in the 1930s was British Palestine, the area known today as Israel. Zionists — Jews who believed they should have a national homeland — successfully urged some German Jews to leave the Third Reich for Palestine. But the German government ordered an end to emigration in 1939 with the outbreak of war. Those who stayed behind in Germany were trapped.

Also trapped were a variety of institutionalized citizens — people who were mentally ill and mentally retarded, among others. Doctors who were loyal Nazis used injections and starvation to kill at least fifty thousand "mental defectives" before German civilians complained to the point that the crusade against these helpless people was halted late in 1940. No "final solution" (the phrase used by the Nazis to mean the plan to exterminate all Jews and other minorities) would be handed down by Hitler's government until 1942. But beatings, killings, and imprisonment in concentration or death camps of Germany's Jewish citizens took place long before war began.

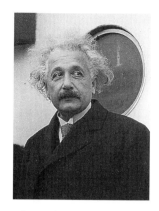

Albert Einstein, a German Jew, fled his native land for the U.S. in the 1930s. Well-known scientists or intellectuals like Einstein were welcomed; more ordinary victims of fascism were not.

A World on the Edge

Hitler's tangle of political and racial views certainly sparked World War II. But other people, nations, ideas, and events played large parts in igniting a war that swept across Europe, Asia, and around the world. Among them:

• The rise of Japan to world-power status. A society shut off from the West until the middle of the nineteenth century, Japan made up for lost time by building modern industries and a huge and efficient military machine. Years before the attack on U.S. forces at Pearl Harbor in 1941, Japanese forces controlled the Korean peninsula, eastern China, various islands, and chunks of Southeast Asia. Democracy had no history in Japan, so there was little debate over the country's far-reaching military decisions.

• The totalitarian government of the Soviet Union. Soviet dictator Joseph Stalin was responsible for the deaths by starvation or imprisonment of millions of Soviet citizens during the 1930s. These horrid events were brought on by the fact that middle-class Ukrainians and others were reluctant to turn over property to the state. Jews and other ethnic minorities were kept from living where they chose in the Soviet Union. They had been confined for decades to Russia's western provinces and parts of Poland, which made later extermination of Jews by invading Nazis easy. Despite a non-aggression pact signed by Hitler and Stalin in 1939 — and later broken by Hitler — mutual distrust between Germany and the Soviet Union made war between the two inevitable.

Joseph Stalin began killing fellow citizens of the Soviet Union in the 1930s and did not let up until Germany attacked the dictator's country in the summer of 1942.

• The inability of World War I's victors to enforce the Treaty of Versailles. Britain and France allowed Germany to rearm, even though rebuilding the German military violated terms of the treaty. By the time British and French leaders saw the danger of the new Germany, the Germans had begun gobbling up foreign territory and war could not be avoided. The United States did not enforce the treaty in part because it had not been treated as an equal by British and French diplomats.

• Bigoted or narrow-minded individuals and groups in many European countries who did Germany's bidding. Fascists in Romania, Hungary, the Balkans, and elsewhere attacked their own minorities with glee, rounding them up for transport to death camps or killing them on the spot. These puppets were as effective in their own brutal way as the many brave resistors who fought the Nazis with nothing but out-of-date weapons and raw courage.

• The virtually worldwide practice of nationalism. Many nations automatically assumed that their view of the world was correct and that others were wrong, inferior, or backward. Strong nationalists were a little too eager to lay their lives — and the lives of everyone else — on the line to save their own country. In contrast, many internationalists — particularly European socialists — believed that all people were equal and that nations were merely created by the convenience of language or geography or shared interests. The years between the two world wars were not prosperous ones for internationalists, since those in capitalist countries such as the United States were often viewed as communists or radicals. The only accepted U.S. internationalists were people who wanted to do more business abroad.

The U.S.A., 1929-1939

Life in the United States was no picnic in the years prior to World War II. The Great Depression began in 1929 and bottomed out in 1932, but jobs were hard to find throughout the 1930s. Grown men really did sell apples on street corners to earn nickels and dimes for their families. Mothers patched together clothing so their children would be presentable at school, and children stuffed cardboard into their shoes when holes wore through the soles. Families ate meals of nothing but bread and milk or coffee. If a teenager could find a job, he or she frequently quit high school to work and help the family.

Many fewer women than men held jobs. Those who were able to find work as professionals were overwhelmingly teachers, nurses, or in other service areas, since these were careers for which women with higher education could successfully compete. For women of working-class or lower economic backgrounds, birth control was seldom practiced or available, resulting in large families and many mouths to feed. Few large families had children who all lived to adulthood. Pneumonia, influenza, polio, tuberculosis, typhus, diphtheria, tetanus, malaria, smallpox, and other diseases killed off some adults and quite a few children. As is often the case, people with the least money were the most often afflicted and least likely to be properly treated.

The Great Depression wore down most Americans, as these Arkansas children prove. The two girls and a boy were found living in an abandoned houseboat with no food, their older brother having deserted them after their parents died.

Suffering during the Great Depression differed a great deal between city and country. Wage earners in the cities who lost their jobs had nothing to fall back on. They needed a steady flow of money to make the monthly mortgage payment, purchase food, buy clothing, and more. Some rural residents, at least those who lived on farms, fared better. They, too, may have skipped an occasional mortgage payment, but a few small-town bankers who knew the farmers personally were willing to give them extra time to make their payments. There was little money in rural areas, but cash was less necessary than in major cities. Farmers could barter cuts of meat or potatoes or baked goods for a visit to the doctor or a new pair of shoes.

A Brutal Time for Blacks. If European-Americans in the United States suffered through the 1930s, African-Americans suffered more. Besides being the first fired and the last hired, few Blacks owned property. Instead, they were often sharecroppers, farmers who raised crops on land owned by others and paid for the use of the land with a percentage of the yield. One problem with this system, of course, is that the landlord is to be paid before the worker takes any of the harvest. In poor crop years, or in areas where cotton was stunted by attacks of the boll weevil, lack of income and near starvation were realities.

African-Americans received little education because most lived in desperately poor, rural, southern areas with no tax base to support their segregated schools. They suffered from anemia, rickets, and even mental retardation due to lack of proper nutrition; they were afflicted with infectious diseases almost unknown to the European-American majority; and their clothing sometimes was made out of woven sacks originally used for animal feed. Blacks also were subjected to very different standards of law enforcement than their white neighbors.

Occasional lynchings took place, not only in the Deep South but in midwestern cities such as Marion, Indiana. Blacks were harassed by a secret racist, paramilitary organization that had emerged in the post-Civil War South and called itself the Ku Klux Klan. A few weeks after the Japanese

Two African-American men, accused of murder, are lynched in Marion, Indiana, in 1930 without a trial. Indiana, though not a southern state, was a center of Ku Klux Klan activity in the 1920s. This brutal event received renewed attention in 1994 following publication of a moving story by a woman who realized that her grandfather, who belonged to the Klan, had been part of the ugly crowd shown here.

A Jewish boy is forced to cut his father's beard as soldiers in Nazi Germany jeer. Jewish persecution took place because the Jews were a minority, they were different from most Germans, and the Nazis needed scape-goats to dominate and abuse.

attack on Pearl Harbor, a mob in Sikeston, Missouri, broke a Black man out of the local jail, dragged him around town tied to a car, and then burned him to death. Such instances were rare but helped prompt rural blacks to migrate to Kansas City, St. Louis, Chicago, and elsewhere, searching for safety in numbers and for jobs made even more scarce by the nation's economy.

Anti-Semitism Takes Root. Jewish-Americans also felt the occasional wrath of the majority. Even though Jews had been quietly kept out of powerful positions in the banking business, many Americans blamed "Jewish bankers" for the Great Depression. Some believed books from the late nineteenth and early twentieth centuries that advanced the notion of Aryan or Nordic racial superiority, while others read auto manufacturer Henry Ford's openly anti-Semitic Dearborn, Michigan, newspaper. The German-American Bund, a group of would-be Nazis under Fritz Kulin, espoused anti-Semitic feelings; however, the Bund and other Nazi groups quickly lost members after the Japanese attack on Pearl Harbor.

The dislike of Jews, while not as rooted in U.S. society as racial prejudice, persisted. Persecution of the Jews in Europe at the time had little positive effect on America's views of its Jewish minority. Many of President Franklin D. Roosevelt's advisors were Jewish, which accounted for some of the opposition to his depression-recovery plan, known as the New Deal. They included Henry Morgenthau, Jr., secretary of the treasury; David Lilienthal, who would become the head of the Atomic Energy Commission; and Bernard Baruch, a financier. Given the fact that there were several Jews so close to the President, it's hard to say why action wasn't taken early to rescue more of Europe's most persecuted people. *Life* magazine, hugely popular at the time, ran photos and stories of Nazi concentration camps long before the U.S. declared war.

Because many American Jews were of European heritage and often had socialist leanings, they joined labor unions. Some industrialists realized this and became more firmly anti-Roosevelt, anti-union, and anti-Semitic. A small number of union members were communists, a fact that frightened owners of business and industry. Some unionists and a few intellectuals continued to espouse communism until learning, usually after World War II, that Stalin had been guilty of his own atrocities.

Nothing reflected the plight of Jews more than a shameful incident in the spring of 1939. A merchant ship, the *St. Louis*, arrived in Cuba carrying 907 German Jewish passengers. These people were on the waiting list to be admitted to the United States and, with their Cuban visas, decided to flee Germany and wait safely in Cuba until called to the United States. But the

Cubans did not recognize their visas and the U.S. would not expand its rigid immigration quota. The ship sailed back toward Europe. Belgium, Britain, France, and the Netherlands eventually absorbed most of the *St. Louis*'s passengers, though a few were returned to Germany and almost certain detention and death.

A Trickle of Migrants

For other ethnic and national groups, times were equally difficult. The immigration quotas, established in 1924, ended legal migration to the U.S. for most Asians. Other groups, particularly Europeans, were given preferential treatment. Just one hundred Chinese a year were admitted from 1924 onward, for example, but at least five thousand Hungarians, many of them Jewish, were admitted between 1935 and 1940. Mexicans were also subjected to very tight quotas, primarily to preserve agricultural jobs in the American Southwest. By 1940, seventy thousand Puerto Ricans were living in the U.S. But the start of World War II meant that German submarines were patrolling the Atlantic coast; that helped shut off further immigration to the mainland from all over the Caribbean.

Americans perceived the position of their prewar country in two ways. Some wanted to follow a path of isolationism, feeling that problems in Europe or Asia were of no importance to the United States. Let's solve our own problems before we sail off to unravel the mess in Europe, the isolationists reasoned. Others saw the rise of fascism in Europe and Japan's moves on the Asian mainland as outrageously provocative behavior, and many African-Americans actively worked to assist Ethiopia after fascist Italy's invasion of that country in 1935. Some Americans pointed to events such as the civil war in Spain in 1936, which resulted in many civilian deaths and the installation of fascist dictator Francisco Franco, as proof that democracy everywhere was in trouble.

There were valid arguments on both sides. The isolationists could reel off statistics showing that ten million adult U.S. males remained unemployed and that the Great Depression was a wound that would not heal. They were conservative and especially strong in the Midwest, where the average citizen disliked talk of a military buildup. That was just another case of the federal government wasting money that could be put to better use, they felt. In words that sound as current as today's news, isolationists did not want their country to become the world's policeman.

Who wanted to get involved? According to surveys, fewer than 10 percent of Americans as late as early 1939 felt the country should actively support threatened nations. Many of these people were first- and second-generation Americans, or they saw Britain and France as longtime allies and Germany as a country under the control of a madman. But even though boatloads of religious and ethnic minorities were fleeing Germany every week, and despite widespread condemnation of Germany's racist policies, little was officially said in the U.S. about Hitler's war on minorities in his own country.

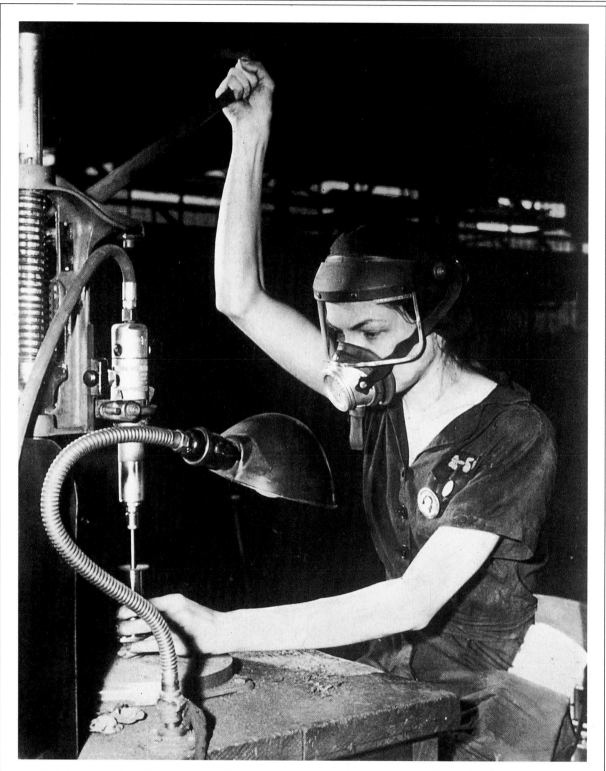

A defense-plant worker operates a drill on the home front during WWII. Millions of American women contributed to the defense effort by taking jobs previously filled by men.

CHAPTER TWO

An "Arsenal for Democracy"

I t was for good reason that John Steinbeck's gritty book *The Grapes of Wrath* was an immense bestseller all across the United States: it was all too true. The book came out in 1939 and told of penniless, desperate, rural Oklahomans driven off their land by soil erosion, drought, and low farm prices. These people of mostly English, Irish, or Scottish heritage, portrayed as heroes and victims, patched together old cars and trucks and hobbled toward California. There, worked harder than human beings should be worked, they were seldom able to afford a permanent roof for their heads. For a few years, they did anything they could to survive.

Despite President Franklin D. Roosevelt's New Deal programs, there wasn't a lot of government assistance for the poor. The best example of a non-government proposal that failed was the "Ham and Eggs" campaign in California and a few other states. This plan promised $30.00 every week ($1,500.00 a year) to unemployed men over the age of fifty. The federal government would get the money from the well-to-do, those whose annual incomes exceeded $3,000.00. Older men demonstrated, chanting "Ham and Eggs!" and "Thirty every Thursday!" to no avail. This proposal and others like it were defeated on the West Coast and in Ohio, Kentucky, Nebraska, and Texas.

Minority suffering during the 1930s defies the imagination. In Houston, for example, neither food nor money was ever available because there would not be enough to go around for all of the white people! Municipal, county, and state relief schemes all across the country were broke by the time Franklin D. Roosevelt took office in 1932. Some women turned to prostitution — they could make $1.50 from one customer, more than could be earned from a day of sewing, cleaning, or processing food. Church was a welcome source of comfort for minority women, but few had decent clothing to wear to religious events. Bootlegging — the production of illegal, intoxicating liquor — became a cottage industry, even after the repeal of U.S. anti-drinking laws in 1934 once again made legal alcoholic beverages available in stores, bars, and restaurants.

An estimated two hundred thousand children were alone and on the road in 1932. Hoboes and transient children and adults were everywhere, their shanties ringing major cities on railroad rights of way and along highways. In one year, one thousand people of all ethnic groups died of malnutrition in North Carolina. Three North Carolina African-American men with jobs stoking the fires on the Atlantic Coast Line Railroad were fired so that the company could keep three European-American firefighters who had less seniority. Eighty percent of the African-American women who found work were employed as domestic servants. The news media didn't help much, since it hinted that seeking relief was an admission of failure. Finally, thanks to a decision made in Washington, D.C., money misery slowly ended.

The decision was made by President Roosevelt. His administration moved in January 1939 to sharply increase the defense budget. He was sure war loomed on the horizon, for allies of the United States if not for the U.S. itself. War did, indeed, begin in Europe that September, and the president declared a national emergency. He decided the following year to send more surplus war materials to Britain and to begin the first peacetime draft. "Okies" and "Arkies," as displaced migrant farmers from Oklahoma and Arkansas were called, were needed in West Coast aircraft plants and by Uncle Sam. Overnight, employment tripled at places such as Douglas Aircraft in Santa Monica, California.

The same know-how that could fix a rusted piece of farm machinery was put to work building glistening, aluminum-bodied planes. Those who showed unusual ability were quickly promoted to supervisory positions. Families that could not afford adequate clothing a few years earlier began to shop for houses as their husbands put in long hours to bring home large paychecks. Many of the men who had passed physical examinations were ordered to report for a year of active military duty in 1940. So families faced only a brief period of economic hardship before husbands would return to high-paying defense jobs — or so they believed. Unfortunately, the plans of Adolf Hitler got in the way, muddling many American lives.

Hitler Incites War

To understand the twisted thinking of Hitler is to understand central Europe in the early twentieth century. Hitler roamed the streets of Vienna as a teenager and fell under the influence of Pan-Germanism, the idea that all German-speaking people should be united in one country. At the time, ethnic Germans could be found in Poland, Russia, Czechoslovakia, Austria, and several other countries. These people had lived away from Germany for

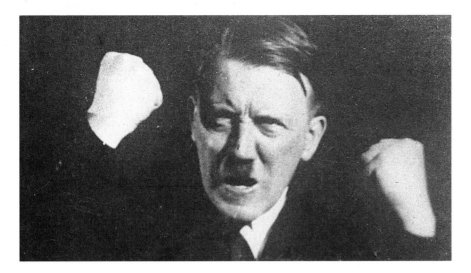

Hitler was a mesmerizing speaker, in part because he put so much emotion into each appearance. He was obsessed with uniting all German-speaking people into a heavily fortified, "racially pure" country that would be the hub of civilization.

centuries, but reuniting them was a popular idea. Hand in hand with one Germany was the move to throw all people seen as "foreigners" off German soil. This included Slavs, Gypsies, and most of all, Jews.

Hitler reports in his autobiography, *Mein Kampf* ("My Struggle"), that Jews were responsible for urban ills in the otherwise wonderful city of Vienna. Several years later, sent to Germany to recover his sight after being gassed by the British in World War I France, Corporal Hitler became convinced that Jews ran the German government. When the government sought peace and then fell apart, Hitler's anti-Semitic views solidified. And when socialists took over a disorganized postwar Germany so that it would have some sort of government, the future dictator's long-standing dislike of anyone who believed in democracy or equality intensified. Many German-speaking people felt as Hitler did, just as some Americans today harbor racist or prejudiced thoughts. Yet not many others showed Hitler's degree of fanaticism.

It is difficult to gauge the feelings of the German people for Hitler and National Socialism (Nazism) as the dictator rose to power. Hitler's early supporters included World War I veterans, traditional German nationalists, industrialists, and other unhappy white-collar Germans who believed social-ism paid too much attention to the needs of workers. While certainly not *every* German citizen shared *all* of Hitler's twisted views, many found them-selves frequently agreeing with the forceful, convincing speeches of the extremist dictator. A historian has said that no one else on earth possessed all of Hitler's poisonous qualities. Sadly, Germany required only one such person to formulate its missions of hate, death, and defeat.

Once in office, Hitler turned Germany into a mirror of his views. The country's two major Christian churches, Catholic and Lutheran, were issued regular orders on all sorts of subjects. Torchlight parades involving huge crowds were capped by the burning of classic books written by world-famous authors whose words failed to align with the Nazis. Signs went up on storefronts all over the country warning Jews that they could not buy milk for their children or drugs for their ill. News and information were delivered

by Nazi papers, radio stations, and films. Germans were no longer offered a range of opinion, encouraging them to think more and more like their demented leaders.

In addition to Hitler, several other Nazis were worth watching. Herrmann Goering was President of the Reichstag and second in command to Hitler. A World War I flying ace, Goering would direct his country's air force (the Luftwaffe) and steal works of art from conquered countries. Paul Joseph Goebbels, colorless and sneaky, was minister of propaganda; he used German movies, radio, press, and theater to stir up hatred agains Jews and other groups. Sadistic secret policeman Reinhard Heydrich would be killed early in the war by anti-Nazi Czechs. Poultry farmer Heinrich Himmler became leader of the group of storm troopers known as the SS and, by the end of the war, directed troops despite having no military experience. Rudolph Hess, Hitler's personal secretary, eventually became second to Hitler in the succession to Nazi leadership. Hess was captured in 1941 in Scotland, where he had flown, supposedly to begin peace talks between Britain and Germany.

Books are burned at a Nazi rally at the University of Berlin in 1933. Hitler ordered the destruction of all books he thought dangerous, and he rigidly censored the press.

Below, left to right: **Hermann Goering, second in command to Hitler; Paul Joseph Goebbels, Nazi Germany's minister of propaganda; Reinhard Heydrich, Nazi secret police official; Heinrich Himmler, head of the SS, a huge group of storm troopers.**

Germany Conquers Europe

The conquest of Europe by the Germans began in the spring of 1938. "To preserve order," Hitler's army marched into Austria, uniting it with Germany. Neither Britain nor France took any action. In the fall of that same year, when the British and French complained about German troops overrunning German-speaking western Czechoslovakia, Hitler signed the infamous Munich Pact with Britain, France, and Italy (the Czechs had no say in the matter). This paper allowed Hitler to keep western Czechoslovakia if he

promised no further aggression. A famous piece of newsfilm shows British Prime Minister Neville Chamberlain stepping off a plane, waving the agreement and promising "peace in our time."

It didn't happen. In the spring of 1939, Germany invaded what was left of Czechoslovakia. Neville Chamberlain later resigned in disgrace and was replaced by Winston Churchill. At about the same time, Italy under fascist dictator Benito Mussolini attacked Albania, Europe's least developed country some 150 miles to its east, across the Adriatic Sea. Earlier, in 1935, Italy had invaded Ethiopia on the horn of Africa near today's Somalia. For the first time in the twentieth century, here was a Black versus white war. African-Americans became active in support of Ethiopia, holding benefits and sending supplies. But the Ethiopians with outdated weapons were no match for Italian tanks and artillery. The country was crushed.

Haile Selassie, who called himself the Lion of Judah and claimed to be a direct descendant of Solomon, king of ancient Israel, and the queen of Sheba. As emperor of Ethiopia, he saw his African nation devoured by Italian troops.

With such trouble brewing, you might think the U.S. would open its doors to refugees. There's no evidence of large Albanian or Ethiopian admissions to the U.S., however. The United States also could have taken in 10,000 homeless German Jewish children at this time, but most Americans felt the U.S. had enough trouble maintaining a decent standard of living for its own citizens and thus opposed the idea. Britain eventually accepted 9,000 of the children, whose parents were imprisoned or in concentration camps; the United States admitted only 240! And yet, only one year between 1933 and 1945 saw the U.S. German-Austrian immigration quota filled. To his credit, President Roosevelt used executive powers to keep in the U.S. 15,000 refugees who were already in the nation on temporary visas.

This dismal record of accepting war refugees left the U.S. with an image of narrow-minded insensitivity that has been difficult to shake to this day. Part of the reason was the growing number of refugees knocking on the country's door for admission — more than could be accommodated in a country with lingering unemployment. Another problem was that many Americans were afraid of letting in spies and saboteurs among the innocent immigrants. An entire wartime publicity campaign revolved around the

Young German fascists are saluted during a Nazi ceremony in 1934. The fanaticism shown by many Germans continues to be a source of wonder and fear to this day.

slogan "Loose Lips Sink Ships": Americans' fear of sabotage was so great that many citizens saw a direct connection between the arrival of immigrants and the fact that the power went off or the well ran dry.

America's Peacetime Draft

Some 16.5 million American men between the ages of twenty-one and thirty-five registered for the draft when it went into effect in 1940 — shortly after Germany had overrun Belgium and the Netherlands. Despite talk of isolationism, only

The children of London are evacuated prior to a German air attack in 1939. Several English cities were heavily damaged, but British victories in the air made Hitler decide against an invasion.

twenty-six males refused to take part in the initial registration! This single-minded view of the military lasted throughout the war: just 5,000 men chose to desert during all of World War II. By comparison, 250,000 men refused to be drafted in World War I. Clearly, the U.S. felt that Germany and Japan were more of a potential threat in 1941 than Germany and Austria had been in 1914. Just as important was the fear that a person in uniform who deserted in time of war might be shot for betraying his country.

Not betrayal but conscience motivated some to refuse military service during the period 1941-45. Among them were members of 152 different religions. A total of 3,562 Mennonites registered as conscientious objectors — people who believe military service would violate their relationship with God. A few Jehovah's Witnesses refused even to sign up for the draft. Such refusal usually resulted in imprisonment. The best-known group of conscientious objectors were Quakers, members of the Society of Friends, a Christian denomination long known for its pacifism. Many Quakers registered as conscientious objectors and ended up working long hours in hospitals and performing other kinds of ill-paid jobs instead of joining the military.

Non-participants in the war were kept in various places, including two camps for conscientious objectors — one in New Hampshire and one in California — and several prisons. A prison in Arizona provided housing for several American Indians who believed the conflict to be strictly a "white man's war." These grandsons of warriors who had fought the U.S. cavalry were mixed in prison among people whose religion would not permit them to fight, as well as people convicted of theft, rape, murder, and other serious crimes.

Women Go to Work

Once husbands, brothers, and boyfriends departed, many American women joined the war effort by getting jobs in defense industries. Arsenals such as the one at Dover, Delaware, preferred to hire women because they felt females were faster and more careful handling potentially explosive material. A total of fifteen hundred Delaware women did everything from operating heavy presses to performing laboratory analyses. Only "bull work" — moving weighty objects — was left to the men.

The defense buildup was welcomed by African-Americans, whose rate of unemployment was much higher than that of European-Americans all over the country. Yet their hopes were dashed as discrimination in defense plants was widespread. A West Coast aircraft factory was typical, posting a notice that "the Negro will be considered only as janitors and in other similar capacities. . . ." The same point of view in government-backed job training existed even after President Franklin Roosevelt ordered an end to discrimination in defense-related matters. That order was issued in 1941 to put off a proposed protest march on Washington by African-Americans.

Earlier, in the late 1930s, Americans had realized that theirs was an ill-prepared military. In time of peace, it was standard U.S. policy not to keep a large standing Army. To save money during the 1930s, the Army had been whittled to the bone — just 186,000 men were in uniform as late as 1939. The Army's primary mission during the Great Depression was to scrimp where possible. Everything from clothing to weapons was of World War I vintage. Helmets were shallow and flimsy "doughboy" models, and there were several stables of horses for the cavalry! Flying was a novelty. In fact, only one American in one hundred had ever flown. Pilots were a wild bunch, traveling all over for races and air shows. Among the best known were Roscoe C. Turner and Hubert Fauntleroy Julian, an African-American who billed himself as the "Black Eagle of Harlem."

The Navy was in better shape, but only in the Pacific was the fleet near ideal strength. Naval forces in the Atlantic relied on the British to control that ocean. One of the reasons for the lack of preparedness was the memory of World War I. Americans believed war solved nothing, so why build arms? One popular view shared by mothers and ministers alike was that

Frances E. Harman, formerly a waitress, drills rivet holes in a Los Angeles aircraft factory. Skirts and dresses were set aside and slacks became popular as women quickly learned assembly-line work in factories all across the U.S.

Rosie the Riveter, an American heroine

Artist Norman Rockwell painted people not as they were but as they should be under the very best circumstances. On May 29, 1943, the cover of *The Saturday Evening Post* was graced by a Rockwell portrait of "Rosie the Riveter."

Rosie was shown eating a sandwich, apparently during lunch break at a defense plant. Her muscles bulged and her figure stretched her coveralls, yet she had an innocent appearance. Her rivet gun, which she used to assemble ships, rested in her lap, and she wore protective goggles propped proudly on her forehead. In a word, she was gorgeous.

Rosie gained fame not only for her looks, but also for what she represented: the women who played a very real part in keeping Allied troops armed

and supplied throughout World War II. More than six million American females from all walks of life constructed ships, loaded shells, sewed uniforms, packed food, and performed many other jobs previously considered "man's work."

Rosie's cover picture was torn from the rest of the weekly magazine and sent overseas to soldiers by working mothers, sisters, wives, and girlfriends. Before the end of the war, everybody knew Rosie! Once the war was over, however, there was a concerted effort by the media to convince women that their appropriate place was back in the home. Working women in huge numbers were laid off and returned to homes, to schools, or to peacetime jobs now that their services were no longer needed.

Among the first African-American pilots was Hubert Julian, shown here in 1939.

military service would turn their Christian sons into sex-crazed killers. The military was held in such low esteem between the wars that officers seldom showed up in public in uniform. With such a poor popular image, it's miraculous that future leaders such as Omar Bradley, Dwight Eisenhower, and George Marshall stayed with the program through the 1930s.

Losses at Sea . . .

The Atlantic Ocean played an important role in bringing the country into the war. Beginning in January 1940, German submarines preyed upon Allied shipping. In the first two months of the year, Nazi torpedoes sank 4.5 million tons of ships sailing between European ports and the United States. From before the U.S. entered the war through the first year of the war in 1942, more U.S. merchant seamen suffered casualties than did U.S. soldiers. Many of these men were either foreign nationals or first-generation U.S. citizens from virtually every seafaring country on earth. Convoys of ships were easy targets, though the British had more surface ships than Germany and always escorted merchant shipping crossing the seas.

Could war have been prevented?

If the U.S. had acted decisively by immediately ordering Hitler and Germany to honor the Treaty of Versailles, would Germany have backed off? Probably not, since the United States simply wasn't the great power in the 1930s that it became by war's end in the mid-forties. Had Franklin D. Roosevelt confronted Germany, it might have seemed no more of a threat than one issued by Canada or Brazil, for example. Britain's navy was larger than the U.S. Navy. France's army was larger than the U.S. Army. Germany's air force was larger than the Army Air Corps. There is no reason to believe that Hitler would have paid attention. He certainly paid little heed late in 1939 to modest U.S. efforts to stop the war following Germany's rapid victory over Poland, its neighbor to the east.

The U.S. might have done more than read headlines and listen to radio broadcasts from Europe if times had been better. Unlike the secretive Soviets, the Germans certainly did not try to hide their government's undemocratic, hate-filled conduct. But some historians argue that the U.S. did not consider involvement in the war until it felt that its economic interests were being threatened. (This occurred when Japan bombed Pearl Harbor as part of its effort to weaken the presence of the United States in parts of Asia.) The U.S. also continued to be absorbed by its own economic problems at home, failing to pay adequate attention to world events until it was too late.

. . . and on Land

Land war actually began in Europe on September 1, 1939, nine days after Hitler and Soviet leader Joseph Stalin signed a secret agreement not to fight each other. Germany then attacked Poland from the west and the Soviet Union invaded from the east a few days later. The British and French, pledged to defend the Poles, declared war on Germany but then did nothing. The Polish military fought valiantly, with weapons from the nineteenth century and World War I against Germany's incredible air power and the Soviets' huge army. German air raids were accompanied by motorized infantry, tanks, and artillery that churned quickly through the Polish countryside. Warsaw surrendered on September 27. Following this *blitzkrieg* (lightning war), the victors divided the country down the middle.

While the fate of Poles at the hands of the Soviets wasn't kind, the Nazis were diabolical. Behind front-line German troops came members of special police and security forces. In some cases too old or physically unfit for combat, these troops marched Jews and others they disliked systematically out of every conquered village. They ordered the captives to dig ditches, then shot them to death and covered the victims with the fresh earth. At least one German general complained to Berlin about such tactics. Leaders of the security forces immediately ordered their troops not to stop the slaughter but to perform it out of sight of the regular army! The torture and killing of Jews, Poles, and others went on and on and on.

Hitler, who personally directed German military strategy and tactics, was not overly anxious to test the military strength of the United States on Europe's western front. But he seemed to want war with everyone else. His army overran Denmark and Norway quickly in the spring of 1940, then looked westward. As it had done everywhere, Germany struck without warning, bombing and killing more enemy soldiers and civilians than was necessary.

A Jewish resident of Germany, like all German Jews at the time, is required to wear a six-pointed star in public. Identifying Jewish citizens made it easy to round them up for transportation to concentration or death camps.

In a matter of days, the Netherlands, Belgium, and tiny Luxembourg surrendered to the Nazis. Hitler had good reason to grab these countries; if they were under Nazi control, German ground forces would not have to face strong fortifications erected by the French. Instead, German soldiers could attack France from the north, through Belgium, moving around one end of the French fortifications.

Thus French and British troops were driven back by German air and ground forces, which rolled through the heavily forested Ardennes area of Belgium, pushing the British in particular toward the sea. Winston Churchill knew that Britain had to act quickly or face losing every soldier at the front. Rallying the Royal Navy, the prime minister also appealed to every private boat owner to cross the English Channel and pick up surrounded troops at a small port in France named Dunkirk.

English civilian sailors with all kinds of boats responded as the British fought the overpowering Germans while withdrawing to the beach. In this way, some three hundred thousand British troops were safely returned to their nation. The British, with little to celebrate, acted as if Dunkirk were a victory. One look at the Dunkirk beach, littered with bodies and equipment, told otherwise. It then took the Germans only seventeen days to conquer France.

Hitler wanted to end all opposition west of Germany so he could advance to the east without having to fight a two-front war. Consequently, as soon as the Germans subdued France, they attacked England. The only thing that saved the British was the twenty or so miles of ocean water between them and the Germans. Hitler had to fight Britain with air power, which he did with a vengeance beginning in July 1940. German bombs over the next four months took an incredible toll on London and other sites, but the Nazis lost seventeen hundred planes to skilled and brave British fighter pilots. The British also bombed several German cities. Failure to control the air made Germany decide against invading England for the time being.

African-Americans and the Military

While the British were fighting for their lives, African-Americans were fighting for their honor. Army enlistments late in the 1930s were limited to four small "Negro" units that had been created immediately following the Civil War. The Navy permitted African-Americans to serve only as messmen — that is, as kitchen workers on ship or shore. The Army formed Black labor battalions whose chores included loading ships and general cleanup. Things were worse in the Marines and in the new Army Air Corps. African-American candidates were completely excluded from flying. When the hero of Richard Wright's 1940 novel, *Native Son*, swears at a plane overhead that he knows is piloted by white men, Blacks everywhere felt the frustration as well.

Once inducted, African-Americans found the country trying to pursue a separate-but-equal policy that was always separate and seldom equal. Black Chicagoans arriving at Camp Shenango in western Pennsylvania were not allowed to use the post exchange (a general store) or the post theater, and there were no separate-but-equal facilities for them, as federal law required at the time. Several African-Americans were shot and killed by fellow servicemen, and others wounded, because they attended a camp movie! Such acts of hostility, including several riots and at least one lynching, took place on many posts and bases but were kept quiet by the military.

Below, left: A Black paratrooper, trained as a firefighter, prepares to jump from a plane over Oregon in 1945. African-Americans frequently chafed for combat following training but were often passed over in favor of white soldiers.

Below, right: Black U.S. troops in Normandy, 1944. African-Americans saw intense action in Italy and France in the final year of the war in Europe.

Perhaps that is why leaders such as Adam Clayton Powell, Jr., and the African-American press were of two minds about war. On one hand, they recalled the performance of African-American runner Jesse Owens in the 1936 summer Olympics in Berlin. Hitler had figured that the Berlin Olympics would be the perfect showcase for Nazi claims to Aryan racial superiority, and Owens's gold medal-winning performance was a source of outrage to Hitler and other Nazis and a cause for both patriotic and ethnic pride among African-Americans. On the other hand, African-American leaders believed that European-Americans in the U.S. practiced their own sort of racial superiority that was displayed more openly by the Germans. Most Black Americans reluctantly concluded that, as bad as things were here, they would get worse if Hitler came to power. Powell, a New York City council member and later a congressman, called for "double victory" over U.S. enemies abroad and racism at home.

Besides African-Americans, the only other segregated Americans were men whose ancestors were Japanese. Every other U.S. minority was integrated into the armed forces, although that integration took several forms. While Mexican-Americans, who had joined National Guard units in large numbers in the 1930s for economic reasons, were on the front lines, other minorities were relegated to noncombat duties. A man of Puerto Rican heritage from New Jersey, for example, might succeed at the Fort Bragg, North Carolina, parachute jump school, only to become a waiter for a group of officers in the U.S. Army's 101st Airborne Division. The message, which was seldom subtle, was that only European-American males had the right stuff for combat.

Jesse Owens, the American track star, embarrassed and infuriated Nazi Germany during the Berlin Olympics in 1936. The African-American won four gold medals, shattering Hitler's notions of German racial superiority.

Learning about the Bomb

Less than a month after the conquest of Poland, Germany's leaders were told that an incredibly powerful bomb could be built by taking advantage of the potential power within the atom. This bomb, scientists reported, would have the explosive force of hundreds of tons of dynamite. The German government learned that such a weapon would take years to develop and thus set the opportunity aside. After all, they reasoned, Germany would soon overrun all of Europe and there would be no need for it. Berlin recognized the power of the bomb three years later, but by then German development was far behind a program in the United States named the Manhattan Project.

Ironically, a Jew who chose to flee Nazi Germany in 1933 got the Manhattan Project rolling. Scientist Albert Einstein told President Roosevelt of the potential of atomic energy, and Roosevelt immediately appointed people to look into it. Once the consensus agreed with Einstein, a crash program began to build such a bomb. Throughout the war, Allied scientists (several of them Jewish immigrants) worked feverishly, worrying that Germany would have the bomb before it could be completed in — and used by — the United States.

U. S. battleships burn out of control following the Japanese attack on Pearl Harbor, Hawaii, on the morning of December 7, 1941. Despite strong hints of an attack or invasion, Americans were taken entirely by surprise.

December 7, 1941, and Beyond

T he sun was peeking above the Waianae Mountains as the families living below began to stir on the warm Sunday morning in early December 1941. Many of the Hawaiians were of Japanese descent; their parents and grandparents had come to the Pacific islands beginning late in the nineteenth century to work on one of the huge sugar plantations. Living in the shadow of several U.S. military bases, these Americans and their children sometimes held two jobs, one in a cane field or a refinery, and one in a military base kitchen, hospital, or officers' club.

Sunday was a day of rest, but the growing drone of low-flying planes awakened the Hawaiians still in their beds. They were used to aerial activity, though they may have noticed that the sound differed slightly and the size of the formation was unusually large. Without warning, the villagers heard explosions from several directions. Southeast lay the huge naval fleet at Pearl Harbor. To the east was an air base, and to the north was an army barracks. Concussion rolled toward them in thunderous waves.

Several neighbors ran into the street. The aircraft, which appeared unfamiliar, continued to fly in from the north in huge formations. Bombs and torpedoes hung beneath their bellies and machine guns sprouted from their wings. After many more explosions, the pilots turned their wrath on the villagers, machine-gunning the innocent as they ran from homes to cars and vice versa. An explosion tore a house-sized hole in the main highway, ripping open a water main and masking the sound of antiaircraft fire from the smoldering bases and ships

New York **World-Telegram**

LATEST WALL ST. PRICES

1500 DEAD IN HAWAII CONGRESS VOTES WAR

Above: Pearl Harbor swept nonwar news off front pages on December 8, 1941.

Below: A Chinese-American welder fears being mistaken for a Japanese at a West Coast shipyard. Americans of Japanese descent were forced into internment camps for much of the war.

hit by the intruding planes. What caused the blast — was it a Japanese bomb or one of the five-inch shells Navy personnel were futilely firing at the climbing planes?

Though it seemed unending to those on the ground, the raid on Oahu and Pearl Harbor on December 7, 1941, by the Japanese military lasted about three hours. The Japanese-American villagers were the first confirmed U.S. civilian casualties in what would come to be known as World War II. The next day, the United States declared war on Japan. But that did not bring back the 2,330 service people or the unsuspecting Hawaiians who died in the attack. Many of the 130,000 Japanese-Americans in Hawaii at the time spent the next day pulling living and dead U.S. sailors from harbor waters.

At least fourteen large U.S. warships, many smaller ships, and numerous planes were damaged or destroyed. The attack paralyzed U.S. air and sea power in the Hawaiian Islands and temporarily allowed Japan to seize military supremacy in the Pacific from the U.S. Some of the damaged vessels, filled with explosives and fuel, burned for two weeks. Approximately three hundred sailors on board the battleship *West Virginia*, which tipped over after being hit, were freed days later when the hull was cut open. In a terrible irony, Japanese-Americans were later suspected of aiding the enemy. Everyone on Hawaii knew the only people passing information to Japan were the Japanese consul and its employees, but in the weeks following the raid on Pearl Harbor, U.S. Navy and State Department officials suggested that such an effective attack could not have been made without some information going to Japan from a variety of sources. According to some officials, this information may have been supplied by Japanese espionage agents listening in on the "gabble" of unwitting Navy wives, letter carriers, milkmen, and patriotic second-generation Japanese-Americans. Other officials flat-out accused Japanese-Americans of lacing Hawaii with one of World War II's most effective networks of espionage and betrayal. Such accusations were unfair, because it has since been proven that no Japanese-American betrayed his or her country at any time during the entire four-year conflict.

Meanwhile, on the mainland, it was afternoon. Large woodgrain Crosley,

Philco, or RCA radios that had been playing music or drama in American living rooms blurted the news that Pearl Harbor had been bombed. The following day, December 8, President Franklin D. Roosevelt asked for and received a declaration of war against the Japanese. A similar declaration against Germany and Italy was made three days later. Meanwhile, some Americans were acting — and overreacting — in a variety of ways.

Reactions to a Sneak Attack

Lights were immediately dimmed along the East and West coasts to prevent any sort of enemy attack. A group of men ranging in age from teens to retirees cleaned rifles and shotguns in Concord, Massachusetts, in preparation for an invasion, while farmers near Puget Sound, Washington, patrolled the beaches with pitchforks, clubs, and guns. In Seattle, a panicky crowd rioted, resulting in the beheading of a Chinese resident who was thought by the rioters to be Japanese. A woman driving on the Bay Bridge between San Francisco and Oakland was shot by a home-defense guard after she failed to stop her car when he waved her down. All over the United States, air-raid sirens were tested, adding to the jitters.

This Philadelphia war map provides up-to-the-minute coverage of the conflict in Europe.

The news media

Radio, America's favorite source of prewar entertainment, became America's favorite news source in World War II. And no wonder: radio could cover changing events better than newspapers. No one exemplified the power of radio more than Edward R. Murrow. His live show, "London After Dark," dramatically reported the Battle of Britain each day for CBS News beginning in August 1940. Murrow's word pictures portrayed the British standing defiantly alone against the Nazi onslaught. Radios had been introduced in cars in the late 1930s. Automobiles with radios blaring could be seen pulling to the curb during some of Murrow's most vivid broadcasts.

Many of the most familiar faces on early television cut their teeth reporting on WWII. Walter Cronkite, CBS-TV's longtime network anchorman, was a war correspondent for a wire service. Charles Collingwood, whose TV career spanned thirty years, beat Allied liberators into Paris in 1944. Lowell Thomas began broadcasting war news as early as 1941 over thirteen TV stations. Among the first nonwar events covered on TV were the Republican National Convention and the World Series, both in 1940. But TV would not invade homes in large numbers until the 1950s. Besides the expense, TV production would have deprived the military of radar, which was built by many of the same companies.

Despite the dramatic appeal of radio and the novelty of TV, for the most thorough coverage newspapers remained immensely popular. Ernie Pyle, WWII's best-known war correspondent, sold millions of newspapers by sending back heart-wrenching pieces about soldiers fighting in the Pacific. One of the few sources for news of common soldiers, Pyle ran lists of the men interviewed and their hometowns at the end of his stories. Though killed by a Japanese bullet in the spring of 1945, Pyle's stories made Americans realize that common people were both the heroes and those who suffered most in time of war.

Newspapers were the mouthpieces of their owners. The Hearst chain of papers advocated locking up Japanese-Americans and blamed the war in Europe on the "rotten" British Empire. The same chain portrayed the zoot-suit riots in wartime Los Angeles as part of a mythical Mexican crime wave. Then, like today, newspapers clearly had their own agendas, agendas that could certainly lend a slant to — and frequently distort — the real life they reported.

Several West Coast cities became convinced that the Japanese were about to attack the mainland. Crowds roved aimlessly in downtown areas, hurling bricks to knock out the twinkling lights on theater marquees. A Japanese family in Los Angeles, dressed in formal attire and on its way home from a wedding, was taken to the county jail by members of the FBI. Teenagers grabbed hunting rifles and patrolled lonely stretches of the Oregon coast, on the lookout for the enemy.

Many Americans' ethnic stereotypes of the Japanese were not just wrong, but dangerous. As a result, Americans on both coasts and in between had greatly underestimated the Japanese prior to World War II. For example, highly placed U.S. government officials truly believed that all Japanese had poor vision, perhaps because the shape of their eyes was different from the eyes of most Americans. Consequently — and incredibly — these leaders dismissed the possibility of the Japanese attacking a distant island or ship as beyond their physical and technical ability. Although there were numerous warnings that the Japanese navy was on the

Top: A trio of Sioux Indian sailors use a cartoon of a Japanese officer as target practice at a California naval base in 1942. Such publicity photos, which seem outlandish today, helped recruit all kinds of Americans for the duration of the war.

Bottom: A Japanese soldier, fangs dripping, is used to remind U.S. workers that mistakes aid the enemy. Making enemy soldiers seem less than human reduced regret over having to kill them.

Ignorance of Japan

If the U.S. agonized over involvement in a European war, it hardly bothered to check on the activities of a militarized Japan. If a war starts when combat troops hit foreign soil, then WII really began in the 1930s with Japan's march onto the Asian mainland. Convinced it was destined to rule a vast Far East empire and lead an "Asian Co-Prosperity Sphere," Japan took the peninsula of Korea and large parts of China, killing ill-equipped soldiers of Chinese warlords and innocent civilians alike. Thousands of Chinese lost their lives in 1937 in cities such as Nanking, which were flattened by Japanese aircraft and artillery.

Throughout the 1930s, Japan's military wiped out whatever targets its government chose. The U.S. reacted by delivering protests to the Japanese embassy, then by refusing to sell Japan raw materials it needed for weapons. The U.S. had watched its role diminish in Asia with each advance by Japan, and so this refusal was both a diplomatic and an economic move that increased the visibility of the U.S. The U.S. embargo gave Japan the excuse it needed to plan the attack on Pearl Harbor. Led by Prime Minister Tojo Hideki, a former general who controlled the army, Japan saw itself locked in a battle for leadership in the Pacific with the U.S., a country it felt had looked down on the Japanese since they began to trade with the West almost ninety years earlier.

prowl, neither President Roosevelt nor any of his advisors took the warnings seriously — or soon — enough to prevent the attack.

At least one warning, that the Japanese might attack on a Sunday, came from military officials as early as August 1941. Another warning, in November 1941, instructed the commander of the Pacific Fleet to remove ships from Pearl Harbor as a way of discouraging a Japanese attack. What might have been the final warning of a

A soldier serving in the Philippines with an all-Puerto Rican American unit teaches a Filipino woman some dance steps during off-duty hours. The men with musical instruments are members of the unit's band. Combat conditions in the Philippines were among the harshest encountered by the U.S. military in WWII.

possible attack was actually about to be delivered as the attack occurred. At about eight o'clock on the morning of December 7, a messenger boy carrying a telegram from officials in Washington, D.C., rode his bike toward the U.S. naval station at Pearl Harbor. The telegram warned the commanding officer to be on the alert for a Japanese attack. But as the messenger approached the naval station, the bombing began; the boy spent the rest of the morning hiding in a ditch as the bombs exploded around him.

After the disaster at Pearl Harbor, American attention was riveted to the Pacific. For almost a year, the news was bad. Japanese forces repeatedly defeated British, Dutch, and U.S. troops, planes, and ships in the western Pacific, capturing the Dutch East Indies (today's Indonesia), landing on New Guinea, capturing Hong Kong, Malaya (modern Malaysia), and Singapore, and invading the United States' large colony in that part of the world, the Philippine Islands. At one point, Japan controlled 10 percent of the earth's surface.

Thousands of U.S. troops, separated from ammunition and supplies by miles of ocean, fought a larger Japanese force for control of the Philippines. This cluster of big islands between Australia and Japan was defended by Army troops under General Douglas MacArthur. The folks at home listened daily as the situation grew worse. The Japanese pushed U.S. forces onto the Bataan Peninsula, then onto a small island called Corregidor. At that point, MacArthur departed for Australia, leaving the surrounded troops in the hands of General Jonathan Wainwright.

The Japanese forced the starving, ill-equipped Americans to surrender after a twenty-seven-day siege. Among those captured were sixty-six female members of the Army Nurses Corps. They were separated from the sick and wounded and interned with other female allies in a Filipino university until early 1945. Male captives were marched down Bataan, bayonetted or beheaded when they fell from exhaustion or lack of water. President Roosevelt defended his strategy to defeat Germany before going all-out against the Japanese. His "fireside chat" on the radio was of small comfort to many relatives who did not learn for months or even years the fate of their

A young Japanese-American from northern California awaits transportation to an internment camp. Not one such person collaborated with the Japanese during the conflict. In fact, a Japanese-American combat unit fighting in Italy was among the most highly decorated of the entire war.

captive loved ones. Though spirits on the home front in 1942 were buoyed by a U.S. bombing attack on Tokyo, Americans of Japanese ancestry would pay for the success of a country they no longer knew.

Detaining Japanese — and Their U.S.-born Children

Anti-Japanese feeling was more likely on the West Coast than the East because people with a view of the Pacific were three thousand miles nearer the enemy. Ironically, before the war, Japanese-Americans were popular among other Americans, who believed they were "most like us," in contrast to people of Chinese descent. But that changed quickly in the face of distant defeat. President Roosevelt responded to the anti-alien mood — much of it stirred up by military and federal law enforcement officials who relentlessly lumped people of Japanese descent into a category of "other subversive persons." Roosevelt issued an executive order that called for the rounding up of all Japanese citizens and their Japanese-American children in coastal California, Oregon, and Washington. In all, approximately 120,000 people of Japanese ancestry were corralled in remote inland camps in California and elsewhere, including the Southwest, the South, and even the Midwest.

This created incredible hardships as the detainees were given only forty-eight hours to make arrangements concerning homes, businesses, and personal property. Many were truck farmers, people who grew vegetables for grocery stores and canning companies. Their fields went untended and were often sold to pay mortgages and taxes. The dozen detention camps themselves were crude, with barbed wire, armed guards, and barracks that were cold in the winter and blazing hot in the summer. Food was of poor quality and all books except religious materials and dictionaries were confiscated. It was called internment, but the people who endured it remember it as ex-convicts recall prison. Not until the war was almost over were these citizens of Japanese descent freed.

Why weren't the Japanese on Hawaii confined? The reasons were more economic than humanitarian. With so many people of Japanese ancestry on Hawaii, the islands' economy would have collapsed. Why weren't German- and Italian-Americans kept in detention? Again, their numbers were large and they were spread all across the U.S. But only German or Italian government employees and their families were rounded up, and they were kept for months in a luxury resort in West Virginia!

Clearly, as evidenced by military communications, government policy, and public attitudes, the anti-alien mood spreading across the nation was based on hysteria and a racist distrust of a group that did not "look like" other Americans. It took surprisingly little time for the Japanese and Japanese-American detainees to become a convenient symbol — a sign of U.S. commitment to winning the war. The casualty in this campaign, however, was human rights.

Once the West Coast Japanese had gone quietly to their substandard camps, members of other groups were carefully examined. Virtually no one defended the rights to freedom of speech or religious belief of Jehovah's Witnesses or Quakers, two groups known for deep-rooted opposition to killing. Three widely spread riots took place in a single day in the U.S. when Jehovah's Witnesses attempted to hand out religious publications door to door. Local governments harassed the Witnesses, charging them licensing fees to recruit new members. Other dissidents were simply thrown in prison, including a young man in New Hampshire who was sentenced to six months in jail for calling a police officer a fascist!

Workplace Hazards

The United States became a more dangerous place for all civilians once war began, in part because inexperienced people were performing perilous work. Hundreds of coal miners, for example, died between 1940 and 1945 as they dug for long hours to supply energy needs for production of war materials. Industrial accidents, many involving women who had joined the work force to help win the war, were commonplace. An ammunition plant in Elwood, Illinois, blew up in 1942, killing 49 people. More than 300 people died in Port Chicago, California, in 1944 with the explosion of a pier. And in Cleveland, Ohio, that same year, a liquid gas tank explosion killed 135 workers.

Railroads helped win the war by moving raw materials to factories and weapons, ammunition, food, and supplies to seaside loading docks. With all the traffic — soldiers mostly used trains to visit their homes or return to their bases — trains became terribly overcrowded and dirty. They also became a source for accidents. The worst wartime rail disaster took place near Philadelphia on September 6, 1943, when seventy-nine passengers died in a massive derailment. Other mishaps killed many soldiers and civilians at railroad crossings and sidings in New York, Ohio, Indiana, Tennessee, Utah, and North Dakota.

Not all deaths at sea were blamed on battle. On December 17, 1944, the U.S. Navy lost three destroyers in a terrible storm that hit the Philippines. Some seventy-six people died in Freckelton, England, in 1944 when a U.S. Air Force B-24 bomber crashed into a school. And in a famous noncombat crash, a U.S. Army B-25 bomber ran into the Empire State Building in New York City on July 28, 1945, killing fourteen. Crowds gathered far below to see the fuselage protruding from the world's tallest building. Earlier in the war, on January 17, 1942, actress Carole Lombard died when a passenger plane crashed west of Las Vegas, Nevada. Lombard was returning from the Midwest to Hollywood

A U.S. Army bomber flew into the seventy-eighth and seventy-ninth floors of the Empire State Building in New York City in 1945, killing more than a dozen people. Accidents and disasters became more common as the war effort intensified.

and husband-actor Clark Gable after appearing at a rally to sell war bonds, saving bonds that helped finance the war.

Japan Rules the Pacific

Death came all too often to the U.S. military during the war in the Pacific. Struggling to put together the fleet battered at Pearl Harbor, the United States Navy under Admiral Chester Nimitz fought the battles of the Coral Sea and Midway in May and June 1942. Although in both cases the United States was on the defensive, the huge air and naval fights saw Japan lose many of its best pilots. Historians believe that the Battle of Midway was the turning point in the Pacific conflict because numerous sinkings resulted in the U.S. and Japanese navies being the most evenly matched since before Pearl Harbor.

In the summer of 1942, the U.S. military launched its first offensive against Japanese forces. Marines and Army personnel on August 7, 1942, attacked the island of Guadalcanal, east of New Guinea. Because Japanese forces were well armed and supplied, the island was not secured until early in 1943. Americans reported being stunned that Japanese soldiers fought until surrounded and out of ammunition, then frequently committed suicide rather than surrender. Some saved a single hand grenade to blow themselves up as G.I.s walked among the fallen foe. Worse, civilians on several islands were urged by the Japanese to take their own lives rather than face vividly described but false accounts of American torture.

The terrible fighting continued on many fronts. U.S. and Australian troops stopped an overland march by the Japanese across the wilds of New Guinea. Other islands were taken at a steep price in lives if the Japanese chose to stand and fight. Occasionally, when an island appeared to be of little value, the Japanese quietly withdrew, leaving only a few of their soldiers. When the U.S. learned of the retreat, it simply bypassed places such as a piece of jungle-covered coral named Truk. A few marooned Japanese soldiers did not leave their hideouts to lay down arms until the 1960s and 1970s!

Throughout the war, white U.S. soldiers frequently said it bothered them less to kill a Japanese than a German because the Japanese were less human! The refusal of Japanese soldiers to surrender fed this kind of thinking, leading to occasional atrocities by U.S. forces in the Pacific. Some Marines and Army infantry personnel cut off and collected the ears of dead Japanese. In contrast, German prisoners of war interned in the United States often were treated at least as well as the West Coast U.S. citizens of Japanese descent who had been confined early in 1942. For example, African-American soldiers told of seeing white soldiers take German POWs for Jeep joyrides in rural Virginia!

Benjamin O. Davis, Jr., the son of the nation's first African-American general, was one of the first five Black pilots to be trained by the U.S. Army for combat. A separate training site for Black flyers was created in Alabama in 1942. The U.S. military remained segregated until the Korean War.

A. Philip Randolph, 1889-1979: civil rights leader

A. Philip Randolph accomplished so much in such a quiet way. The son of a Methodist minister, he was born in Florida but moved to the Harlem section of New York City as a young man. He attended City College of New York by night and by day worked to organize fellow African-American workers so that they could enjoy equal rights.

Randolph affected U.S. involvement in World War II even before it began. As president of the Brotherhood of Sleeping Car Porters, he ran the first successful Black union and steered the group in 1938 away from the American Federation of Labor (AFL) and into the more progressive Congress of Industrial Organizations (CIO).

As war began to brew in Europe and the Pacific, he warned President Franklin D. Roosevelt that he would lead a protest march involving thousands of African-Americans upon Washington, D.C., unless discrimination by companies with defense contracts ceased. Randolph would not budge on the issue, and so, on June 25, 1941, the president issued an executive order barring discrimination not only in defense industries but in federal bureaus as well. The order also created the Fair Employment Practices Committee, which enforced the order.

After the war, Randolph's persistence persuaded President Harry S. Truman to integrate the armed forces. An executive order issued on July 26, 1948, banished armed forces segregation ever since.

The tall, thin man updated his pre-WWII promises in 1963 by organizing the March on Washington for Jobs and Freedom. His action brought more than two hundred thousand people to the capital on August 28, 1963, a milestone in the civil rights movement.

Black Pilots, Black Soldiers

Well before Pearl Harbor, there were hints that war lay ahead. A very small one was dropped in 1939 when the Civil Aeronautics Authority, a government agency, began to accept African-American students for pilot training. The program graduated several hundred qualified pilots, the first five of whom came from a special Army flight school at Tuskegee Air Field in Alabama in 1942. Among the five new pilots was Benjamin O. Davis, Jr., an Army officer and the son of the United States' only Black general at the time.

For a time, the conservative military ignored a mandate from Congress ordering that qualified African-American candidates be trained in flight school. The Army Air Corps eventually accepted applications in March 1941, and the final tally was 992 Tuskegee graduates, half of whom were sent overseas. In one of the most successful programs of the war, Black pilots downed 111 enemy aircraft, destroyed 150 aircraft on the ground, sank a destroyer, flew about 15,000 missions, and were awarded an estimated 150 Distinguished Flying Crosses.

In contrast to the opportunities African-Americans had to perform in the military was the lack of opportunity in the civilian world. During the Great Depression, for example, the work force at New York City's electrical utility numbered 10,000, yet only 213 were Black. As early as 1937, African-Americans asked President Franklin D. Roosevelt to remove discrimination in the armed forces so that opportunity would indeed be equal. Except for a token executive order, Roosevelt and his generals paid little attention to the plea, putting European-American officers in charge of African-American soldiers throughout the war. Even on the streets of Harlem, Black residents could only buy daily newspapers from white vendors. Obviously, U.S. society was still dominated by the European-American majority on virtually every level.

Dorothy Mae Hill, left, a Seneca Indian, is greeted by a WAVE officer as she reports for duty in 1943. Twelve thousand women served in uniform in the U.S. Navy during the war.

White soldiers outnumbered Black soldiers by more than ten to one in Europe during World War II. Yet four times as many African-Americans were executed by the government after military trials, called courts-martial. African-American soldiers in England often were accused of sexual assault when they merely attempted to socialize with English women. A total of seventy Americans in Europe during the war were executed by their government — fifty-five were African-Americans, and fifteen were white. In all cases, the crimes were terrible. But there is no way of knowing if many other white Americans escaped execution for similar misdeeds. African-American soldiers who thought things would get better after they were shipped overseas were often wrong.

WACS, WAVES, and Others

Just as the military made grudging room for African-Americans, it gave in to the desire of women to serve. On May 22, 1942, the U.S. Army began taking applications for female officers. It needed only 440 candidates but was swamped with 13,208 applications! A Gallup Poll at the time showed the nation to be ahead of the government in this area; an overwhelming number of Americans felt it better to draft an unmarried woman than a married man who had children. No woman was ever drafted, but a number did indeed enlist.

Unfortunately for the planners, enlistments did not match expectations over the course of the war. The U.S. forecast that 150,000 would join the WACs, or Women's Army Corps, but the number never exceeded 60,000. The WAVES (Women Accepted for Volunteer Emergency Service) of the Navy numbered 12,000. They were required to have college degrees and their officers were graduates of training programs conducted on two college campuses. Marine women numbered 12,000.

Joining the WACs lost its appeal for several reasons. Many women with special skills simply felt that they were qualified to do more than march, exercise, scrub floors, or work in a kitchen. One major source of unhappiness with the military were the ugly rumors of wild sexual activity that followed WAC recruits. Clearly, there was a double standard for males and females wearing U.S. uniforms, and rather than subject themselves to this kind of insult, many women realized they could contribute to the war effort by working for the Red Cross, signing on with the American Women's Volunteer Service or the American Legion Auxiliary, or spending time at the local USO (United Service Organization), a string of wholesome spots that served coffee and doughnuts and tried to remind men of home and family.

Hitler, the U.S., and the Soviet Union

Even before the U.S. declared war, Hitler was worried about the United States. To avoid fighting on both the eastern and western European fronts, he told his generals, Germany should quickly defeat the Soviet Union to the east. Then, when and if the U.S. came to Britain's aid to the west, Germany would be ready. To the dictator's dismay, however — and despite his grand plans — Hitler was not able to count on his friends for support. Franco, the Spanish fascist, wanted huge colonial territory in Africa before sending troops anywhere. The French who answered to Hitler spoke ill of the British but did little else. And Hitler could not share secrets with Mussolini for fear that the Italian royal family would pass them on to the British!

The unpredictable nature of warfare struck Hitler in 1941 when his trusted secretary, Rudolph Hess, took off for Scotland in a fighter plane! Hess believed he could prevent war with Britain, so he ditched the plane, parachuted onto British soil, and demanded to talk to English royalty. Hess told authorities that Hitler did not want to attack England and that, if Churchill and his government were replaced, Germany would make war elsewhere. The British found Hess to be deranged, though they were delighted that he had become an embarrassment to Hitler. Hess was treated as a prisoner of war, escaping a death sentence because of his mental illness.

Rudolph Hess, Adolf Hitler's secretary, believed he could prevent a German invasion of Great Britain. He parachuted into Scotland in 1941, demanding to speak with British royalty.

Other unpleasant surprises awaited Hitler. From Albania, Mussolini attacked Greece. His forces were sent reeling by tough Greek mountaineers who hid in the craggy passes to pick off Italian troops. Hitler was thus forced to attack Greece from Bulgaria to save Mussolini's men. He did the same thing in North Africa, where a ragtag British force of thirty-one thousand, many of them Indian, took on an Italian force of ninety thousand and managed to prevail, ending up with thirty-eight thousand prisoners of war. At such a rate, Italy would soon be out of the war and Germany would have even fewer friends. Though the Nazis had presented enough of a threat to the Soviet Union for that nation to sign a non-aggression pledge with Germany two years earlier, the Soviets traded intelligence with Britain and eventually joined the Allies in their fight against Germany. Hitler's already short list of friends would soon be reduced to only one: Japan.

Survivors of Dachau, the Nazi death camp, peer from behind barbed wire on being liberated in May 1945. Millions of Jews, Slavs, Gypsies, Poles, communists, and the stubbornly religious perished in German camps.

CHAPTER FOUR

War Abroad, War at Home

I f there was one turning point in World War II, it occurred near where two continents, Europe and Asia, meet. Hitler's huge army had overrun Poland, Denmark, Norway, the Netherlands, Belgium, and France. Courageous British flyers held off their German foes, forcing the dictator to postpone the invasion of Britain, though the German army probably could have landed in England even if it might not have been able to conquer or hold the entire island. With his forces in control of France, Hitler turned to the east and the Soviet Union, where he envisioned a vast area for Germany devoted to farming and slave-produced oil and other raw materials.

For weeks in the spring of 1941, the Soviets had received hints of a German invasion, but either leader Joseph Stalin did not want to believe the truth or his aides were afraid to tell him, since he was known to have killed anyone who brought him bad news. On June 22, 1941, the bad news began before dawn as German artillery and air power hammered the surprised Soviets, and German troops overran Soviet forward positions as they entered the Soviet Union.

The invasion was hundreds of miles wide and involved hundreds of thousands of troops. Germans poured through the Baltic states of Latvia, Lithuania, and Estonia toward the Soviet Union's huge northern city of Leningrad. They raced out of Poland and headed for Moscow, the nation's capital. And they swung south, toward the major cities of Kiev, Kharkov, Stalingrad, and the fertile Crimea. Hitler ordered his troops not to let up until they reached the shores of the Volga River, which historically served as the dividing line between Europe and Asia. He planned to control an area almost the size of the U.S. that ran from Archangel, east of Finland, to the Caucasus Mountains, which separated the Soviet Union from Turkey and Iran.

The Germans drove mercilessly eastward, surrounding hundreds of thousands of Soviet soldiers. Behind them came the SS, pulling Jews, various Asians, and anyone else they considered offensive to their vision of Aryan supremacy from among the clusters of helpless civilians and captured soldiers. These prisoners were killed immediately, usually by

machine guns. The remaining civilians were rounded up to meet Germany's labor shortage and put on trains headed west. Parents were separated from children; elderly people were shot or were left to wander and starve. Soviet soldiers who were captured and not immediately gunned down were kept in the open to die of thirst, starvation, or disease. The situation became so desperate that some prisoners ate their dead comrades.

A German motorized unit stalls in snow on the Eastern Front. The weather helped halt, then turn back, Hitler's huge invasion of the Soviet Union. By the end of 1942, many of the surviving German soldiers were in frozen retreat.

Guerrilla Warfare

As German troops neared Leningrad and Moscow, Soviet guerrillas attacked supply trains headed for the front. These fighters behind German lines bedeviled Hitler's forces all the time they were anywhere east of Poland. Not even mass executions of innocent civilians stopped the ethnic Caucasians, Tartars, Russians, and Belorussians. Ironically, had the Germans treated the various Soviet Union ethnic groups with some consideration, they might have joined the Nazis to rid themselves of Stalin and communism. But they quickly realized they were combatting a more fearsome enemy even than Stalin and so put up the fight of their lives.

The Germans surrounded and attempted to starve Leningrad into submission, and they got within sight of the spires of Moscow's Kremlin. But during this drive, Russia's October rains began and German armor, cavalry, and supply vehicles bogged down. After the rains came snow, propelled across the seemingly endless plains and falling for days at a time. The Russian winter arrived early in 1941, and temperatures below zero were recorded in November. The Germans were unprepared for such weather and suffered massive cases of frostbite. Meanwhile, Siberian soldiers and other Soviet ethnic groups around Stalingrad who were more used to the weather bundled themselves and attacked the Germans with everything they had. For the first time ever, Nazi soldiers retreated.

The Soviets launched their biggest counterattack just west of Moscow on December 6, 1941, the day before the attack on Pearl Harbor. The fighting occurred in a snowstorm as troops on both sides fought the weather and one another. Meanwhile, Germans in North Africa were experiencing defeat in a far different climate. British troops, which included Australian, Canadian, and Indian forces, after being pushed across the southern Mediterranean coast, overwhelmed German and Italian forces at a place named El Alamein. Following this struggle, the Allies began to plan the invasion of Italy.

Americans Around the World

Because the war truly was worldwide, all kinds of Americans soon found themselves in all kinds of places. When the Soviet Union attacked its small neighbor, Finland, in 1939, Finnish-Americans scrambled to New York

City and sailed across the northern Atlantic to aid uncles, aunts, and cousins. Numerous American men of Greek descent visiting from the U.S. were unable to leave Greece after Italy attacked and were drafted into the Greek military. At home, Greek-Americans formed the Greek War Relief Association, sending an astonishing $100 million in goods via the Red Cross to their former homeland in neutral Sweden's ships.

One man in five in the U.S. Army in 1939 was of Polish descent, and Poles led Chicago's numerous ethnic groups in the purchase of war bonds. Mexican-Americans enlisted in large numbers. New Mexico's National Guard units, made up primarily of Mexican-Americans, played a major role in the eventual liberation of the Philippines' Bataan Peninsula under General MacArthur. The 88th Division "Blue Devils," many of them former National Guardsmen and of Mexican descent, were the first Allies to arrive in Rome in 1944. And some 215 men from California, whose ancestors came from India, found themselves all over the map—except in India or anywhere in Asia—during the conflict.

Apparently the U.S. government felt that many Asian-American troops would be more effective if they did not have to fight on Asian soil. The exclusion of soldiers from battle based on race or ethnic background is a sad sign of the narrowmindedness that pervaded the U.S. military, especially given the fact that millions of soldiers of European-American descent were shipped to Germany, Italy, and France. With such an attitude underlying its policies, it's small wonder that the military felt it could not "trust" loyal Japanese-American citizens following the attack on Pearl Harbor.

Many young soldiers sent to the four corners of the world were those who were least used to travel. One poor, rural Indiana native who had not left the county of his birth by the time he had graduated from high school was accepted for flight training. The Hoosier was sent to Alabama, Mississippi, and California before flying to the northeast coast of South America. From there, he and his crew flew their B-17 bomber east to North Africa, where they fought Italians and Germans under General Erwin Rommel, nicknamed the Desert Fox. After seeing action as far east as Egypt and Palestine, the pilot was sent to England and then France following the Allied invasion of continental Europe. He returned to the U.S. in 1945 with memories of at least three continents.

Americans from all ethnic groups distinguished themselves in various battles and campaigns. Sabu Dastagir, an East Indian Muslim, was a star in

Top: Finnish soldiers on bicycles leave Helsinki for the front. The Soviet Union invaded Finland in 1939, only to find the Finns a formidable foe. Though the Soviets eventually won part of Finland, they suffered numerous casualties in the far-north forests of their small neighbor.

Bottom: Greek mountaineer troops such as these beat up Mussolini's Italian army when it attempted to attack their country from Albania. Hitler was forced to alter his military strategy to rescue the Italians, which affected conduct of the war in the Soviet Union.

such prewar films as *Elephant Boy* and *The Jungle Book*. He enlisted in the Army Air Corps, was granted U.S. citizenship, and flew forty-two aerial missions as the gunner on a B-24 bomber over the South Pacific. His heroism earned him the Distinguished Flying Cross. Greek-American Christos Karaberis won the Medal of Honor in Italy for wiping out five machine-gun positions, killing eight enemy soldiers and capturing twenty-two. Theodore Kalakuka became the first Ukrainian-American to graduate from the West Point Military Academy. He was captured in the South Pacific and died of malaria in a Japanese prison.

No matter where a G.I. might hope to end up, he was sent somewhere else. W. T. Basore, from Oklahoma, found himself on a remote island south of Burma (modern Myanmar) in the Bay of Bengal. As a private first class, he worked as a mechanic by day and found time to explore by night, riding slowly on a noisy, Army-issue motorcycle with no headlight that nevertheless frightened away curious cows and jackals. Other veterans, now retired, can cite similar experiences in Iceland or China or the Middle East. Civilian government workers also are full of tales, frequently from cities not in the path of fighting, and therefore full of spies and intrigue, such as Beirut, Rio de Janeiro, and Lisbon.

Above: Sabu Dastagir, an American of East Indian Muslim descent, starred in several movies before World War II. As a young man, he flew heroic missions in the Pacific.

Below: Indian Scouts such as these helped the U.S. in the South Pacific by talking in code in their native Navajo as they directed artillery and air strikes.

War in the Pacific and the Navajo Code Talkers

Americans assigned to the Pacific felt they had drawn the low card in the deck. They didn't always have adequate ammunition or supplies, and no one back home knew for sure where they were. Yet with each amphibious attack on a Japanese-held island, U.S. forces became more efficient. At first, there was little coordination between assaulting troops and their air power or naval guns. One result was needless death and injury of Marines and Army soldiers, hit by their own "friendly fire" because they could not report their progress to comrades firing artillery or dropping bombs. Eventually, radio communications improved, but radios brought up another problem: the Japanese

understood English and could eavesdrop electronically on radio transmissions. A solution emerged from an unexpected source — a group known as Navajo code talkers.

The Americans broke Japan's secret code early in the war, then feared that Japan would do the same thing to them. Whether speaking in code or in English, the U.S. military did not want to be overheard. To the rescue came one of the country's largest American Indian groups, the Navajo. Members of this Southwest Indian nation transmitted information to each other in their own language, puzzling the Japanese, who had never heard a tongue like native Navajo.

This was no happy accident; military personnel recruited young men fluent in both English and Navajo off the reservation. Before the war in the Pacific came to an end, more than four hundred Navajo code talkers were using radios to relay secret orders, call in air strikes, and caution shipboard personnel when aiming artillery. The Japanese eventually found someone to help them understand the code, but their effort failed because the native words had been assigned hidden meanings.

Code talkers went through U.S. Marine boot camp, then received additional communications training. Usually, two code talkers were assigned to each division of about ten thousand soldiers. One went ashore with the attacking forces and one stayed on board ship. They communicated with hand-held radios, frequently sending messages while under intense fire and performing all of the other terrible duties that front-line fighting requires. Eleven code talkers were killed in action.

Above: A code talker in 1943. The Japanese eventually found someone who could translate the language, but they never broke the Navajos' code.

Below: Jacqueline Cochran recruited Women's Airforce Service Pilots (WASPs).

WASPs and Other Female Fliers

Another group of U.S. citizens as necessary as the Navajo gave equally of themselves. These were women pilots, 1,074 in all, who were members of the Women's Airforce Service Pilots, or WASPs. These professional pilots were recruited from all across the country by a pioneering air racer named Jacqueline Cochran. She singlehandedly talked the U.S. Army Air Corps into letting women fly ferrying missions at home so male pilots could fly war missions overseas. Not that the WASPs' jobs were easy; they frequently found themselves in new and untried planes that had just been pushed out the factory door. WASPs also carried out such dangerous chores as towing huge strips of cloth to provide antiaircraft gunners with target practice, and they flew planes too old for service to distant junkyards.

The very first U.S. females to fly for their country were twenty-five members of the Women's Auxiliary Ferrying Squadron (WAFS). They successfully trained at New Castle, Delaware, and included one pilot who had 2,950 hours in the air as a stunt flyer and instructor. At about the same time, a few American women joined British volunteers as ferry pilots in Britain, flying new aircraft from factories to squadrons.

These women came from all walks of life. In fact, the only things they had in common were that they were all white and

Hauling their parachutes, WASP flyers leave a hangar in 1943. The pilots ferried aircraft between factories, hangars, and air fields, freeing male pilots for combat duty.

they loved to fly. From a stack of applications that reached 25,000, the top 1,830 candidates were sent to be trained at Avenger Field in Sweetwater, Texas. "Sent" makes it sound as if the government paid their way to the lonely area of western Texas. In reality, all of the women had to use their own money for train or bus fare. Nevertheless, 1,000 graduated from the program.

WASPs ended up flying every kind of craft the United States made, from the huge, four-engine B-29 bomber to the sleek, quick, and deadly P-51 Mustang. Thirty-eight WASPs gave their lives as ferry pilots, logging more than sixty million miles through December 1944, when their services were no longer needed and they were suddenly cut loose without the benefits or formal recognition given to war veterans. Most considered themselves lucky if they could catch flights back to their hometowns. Not until 1979 did Congress recognize WASPs as veterans of World War II, with all of the usual honors and benefits.

There were other female citizens flying for other countries, especially the Soviet Union. At the height of battle on the eastern front in 1942, the United States rushed new aircraft to Alaska. The Soviet pilots who showed up to fly the planes westward were Soviet women — including one who was five months pregnant! Several Soviet females saw combat as pilots, and a navigator, Polina Gelman, left her studies at Moscow University to fly hundreds of bombing missions. A Jew, Gelman had more reasons than most aviators to attack German forces.

As the war dragged on, many unusual combat schemes were considered, and a German woman came up with one of the wilder ones. Test pilot Hanna Reitsch, visiting Hitler in 1944 for a medal presentation, suggested recruiting a

Amelia Earhart, 1898-1937(?), pioneer aviator

Amelia Earhart may have been the first American killed by the Japanese in World War II. Japan was already at war in China when Earhart, an internationally known pilot, left California to fly westward around the world.

She was accompanied by navigator Fred Noonan in her twin-engine Lockheed. Neither was ever seen again, though there is some evidence that the plane was ditched near Howland Island in the southern Pacific Ocean in an area controlled at the time by the Japanese. There has even been speculation that Earhart and Noonan were spies and that they were killed as such by Japanese soldiers.

Earhart was the first female to fly alone over the Atlantic Ocean and the first person to fly alone from California to Hawaii. In her hands and in the hands of other pioneering pilots, the airplane became much more than a novelty; it may also have evolved into a weapon of war, though there is no proof she was ever involved in spying or other warlike activity. A native of Atchison, Kansas, she was married in 1931 to publisher George Putnam but decided to keep her own name, which was already well known.

special group of pilots for suicide planes. These "human glider-bombs" would be aimed at Allied targets and the pilots on board would be sure they scored bull's-eyes, even though the flyers themselves would not live to tell about it. Hitler dismissed the idea but later authorized limited work on the design of such an aircraft. Reitsch was among the first to volunteer for this extreme service to her country, a service the Japanese kamikaze pilots performed late in the war.

Women played more practical roles elsewhere. Yugoslavian partisan leader Josip Broz, known to his comrades as Tito, offered this down-to-earth advice to a woman: "You want a weapon? Go out on the road and take one from a German!" Numerous partisans, many of them women, followed Tito. No conflict saw more women actually fighting than did the savage guerrilla war waged in the mountainous Balkans. Aware that the Nazis would retaliate by executing innocent villagers, Tito's partisans nevertheless ambushed Germans every chance they got, attacking in the open only when they greatly outnumbered the better-equipped Nazis. Women fought with and fell with the men in this campaign, which took place over some of Europe's most rugged terrain.

A Yugoslav partisan fighter, who happens to be female, is offered a cigarette by a British Royal Air Force officer somewhere in the woman's native land. Women under guerrilla leader Marshal Tito received no special treatment and fought valiantly alongside their male compatriots.

Partisans, Guerrillas, and Irregulars

While there were partisan fighters everywhere in Yugoslavia, virtually every conquered country had behind-the-lines heroes fighting on their home soil, including the following:

France. *Maquisards* (irregular forces named for a group of Corsican bandits) numbered almost 150,000 people by D-Day (June 6, 1944, the day of the Allied invasion of Normandy, France). General Dwight D. Eisenhower said these shadowy figures were worth six divisions for the way they disrupted German communications and transportation. Many were deserters from the German-controlled Vichy French occupation army.

Poland. Some 380,000 partisans were bedeviling the Germans by 1944, while an entire Polish army fought alongside British forces through Italy and then into France. Poles who were agents of the Germans fared badly when caught by the irregulars. In the first half of 1944, a total of 796 were executed by fellow Poles as traitors. The Poles also assassinated German Major General Kutschera, executing him in front of Warsaw SS headquarters in broad daylight.

One group of Warsaw fighters showed a special kind of bravery in the face of certain defeat and death. These were members of the Jewish resistance in the Warsaw Ghetto. This prisonlike city-within-a-city was built by Nazi invaders to isolate Jews from other citizens of Poland's capital city — and to provide a point of departure to the death camps. With three hundred thousand Jews from the Warsaw Ghetto deported to the Treblinka death camp in 1942 alone, Jewish fighters chose certain death through resistance over systematic extermination. The Nazis killed the ghetto's remaining inhabitants following the 1943 uprising.

Czechoslovakia. Earlier in the war, Czechs ambushed and killed Hitler's friend Reinhard Heydrich, a cruel executioner who had been sent to Czechoslovakia to quell Czech sabotage and other acts of resistance to the Nazis. Nazi retribution was swift and terrible. Following the shooting of innocent families, a huge reward was offered for information leading to the capture of Heydrich's assailants. When this failed, the Nazis chose to make an example of Lidice, a tiny village apparently chosen at random. On June 9, 1942, again with no evidence that anyone was hiding Heydrich's assailants, SS troops descended on the village and gathered the entire population in the village square. There they lined up and shot all the men, separated the surviving women and children and sent them to concentration camps, and destroyed their homes. When the terror had ceased, not a living soul remained in Lidice. While the world responded with horror to these atrocities, Heydrich's death also sent the message that no German was safe in occupied territory.

Austria. In 1938, Hitler fulfilled his dream of "reuniting" German-speaking Austria with Germany — a goal shared by some Austrians and resisted by others. Anti-Nazi resistance in Austria was seriously hampered both by the incredible military might Germany used to accomplish its objective and by the many Nazi secret agents planted among the Austrian citizenry. But some Austrians did resist, although it took only a few days for Germany to conquer its southern neighbor. Communists were the first to resist Hitler following Germany's reunion with Austria. The Nazis were also resisted by Austrian Slovenes, an ethnic minority targeted by the Germans for relocation.

Crete. The Nazis knew how dangerous female partisans could be: some five hundred were shot by firing squads in May 1941 after German forces overran the island. Germans had forced every able-bodied woman to remove her blouse to search for telltale bruises caused by the recoil of rifles. Those who were bruised were executed as the surviving Crete men took to the island's many hills.

The Netherlands and Norway. Dutch and Norwegian partisans raided Nazi installations in their respective nations, disrupting German communications by destroying telephone and electrical lines, and sometimes killing Nazi soldiers and dumping their bodies into waterways where they wouldn't be discovered.

China. More than one hundred thousand troops surrounded a large group of Chinese partisans in 1938, but the guerrilla fighters seemed to have disappeared. Only later did the Japanese discover that townspeople had constructed a series of tunnels where huge numbers of partisans could hide. Before war's end, tunnels were extended from one village to the next, greatly improving escape and evasion for snipers and others bent on disrupting Japanese forces.

Germany. Late in the war, at least one German general attempted to organize a patriotic underground German army, and a group of officers attempted unsuccessfully to assassinate Hitler (see Chapter Six). Many German citizens certainly disapproved of the Nazis' political and military goals. Some resisted Hitler in word and deed, often by helping Jews escape or even by hiding them in their homes; many more were seduced by the power of Hitler's words or frightened into silence. But most German citizens who followed the dictates of their Nazi leaders seemed more comfortable taking orders than fighting under the loose spontaneity of guerrilla warfare. Perhaps that is why Nazis who survived and were put on trial as war criminals believed that "just following orders" was an adequate defense for their savagery.

(see Chapter Six)

The "Final Solution"

The Germans documented virtually every order they ever gave, which is why historians know so much about the inner workings of the Nazis and the German military. Apparently they were so certain they would win the war they never considered that such written records could be used against them if they lost. It was no secret that Hitler, his friends, and his military leaders had mapped out a series of "solutions" to Germany's "Jewish problem" that included mass resettlement, imprisonment, and deportation. And as the goal of ridding Germany of its Jews expanded to include Jews living beyond Germany's borders, Hitler and his associates talked with increasing openness about a "final solution" to the Jewish population remaining in Europe. In 1942, 80 percent of Germany's Jewish prisoners were still alive. A year later, only 20 percent were left alive, leaving no doubt that the goal of the "final solution" discussed by the Nazis was the killing of every Jew in Germany or in German-held territory.

Most Jews who had not been executed by 1942 had been transported to one of a hundred concentration camps. Early in the war, the diabolically efficient Nazis had constructed special enclosed trucks that could be driven off with the truck's exhaust gases piped into the trailer, which was packed with Jewish prisoners. To the Nazis, the problem with this method of killing was that it took too long and did not kill large enough numbers.

Below: Two British soldiers examine one of three ovens used to kill death-camp inmates in Holland.

Bottom: These ovens in Weimar, Germany, contain the bones and ashes of anti-Nazi German women. U.S., British, and Soviet soldiers were stunned at the huge numbers of victims – and at the careful records kept by the Nazis, who assumed until it was too late that they would win the war.

Consequently, gas chambers were built within the barbed wire of many camps. The Germans burned the gassed victims in nearby crematoria — simply because so many were being killed that they could not be otherwise disposed of.

These camps ceased being "concentration" camps where large numbers of civilians existed under conditions that were merely brutal. They became death camps — factories of death and human destruction where victims were systematically executed and put to ghastly use even after death, when human hair could be turned into wigs and human fat rendered into lard.

How could this happen? As shocking as the killing is the realization that large numbers of apparently sane German soldiers stood by while mass exterminations took place. These soldiers rifled the clothing of the victims and picked watches, rings, and jewelry off dead bodies, sending the material to be deposited in accounts at German banks. Again, the banks kept records. At one camp, breaks occurred between gassing and burning so that German soldiers, dentists, or prisoners could yank gold fillings from the mouths of the dead.

Jehovah's Witnesses and Nazi persecution

The Jehovah's Witnesses faith was founded in the 1870s in New York City. Witnesses preach the belief that the coming of the messiah is close at hand and with it the end of the world as we know it. During World War II, many of their European members died at the hands of German Nazis.

Nazis were avowed enemies of Witnesses for three reasons: the Witnesses were strongly linked to the United States; their opposition to Hitler and National Socialism was unbending; and they refused to be inducted into the military or to work in the German arms industry. As early as 1938, the sect was outlawed in Germany. Despite the ban, Witnesses continued to distribute printed material smuggled in from neutral Switzerland while refusing to vote, observe racial laws, or bear arms.

A law passed on August 17, 1938, made refusal to join the armed forces punishable by death. Convictions of Witnesses before German civilian courts became virtually automatic, despite their oft-cited Biblical admonition, "Thou shalt not kill." Among 417 of their German ministers, 156 were executed. Others were imprisoned or sent to concentration camps.

The harassment of Witnesses took place in German-occupied territory, too. In the tiny village of St. Martin, Austria, twelve of twenty-four Jehovah's Witnesses were executed and all but four were driven from their homes at some time during the war. Persecution began to decline in 1942 as the war tilted in favor of the Allies, though many members were arrested, freed, and re-arrested repeatedly throughout the conflict.

Opposite page, top: Women at the Bergen-Belsen, Germany, death camp use shoes of the dead for fuel to heat water and cook. The Allies overran the last camp in May 1945.

Opposite page, bottom: These gaunt men are slave laborers in their barracks at Buchenwald. Only the heartiest survived long hours of labor and little or no food.

Left: These Jewish women in ill-fitting clothes were tattooed by the Nazis for identification purposes. The German arms factory in which they worked was liberated by U.S. troops in April 1945.

Below: Concentration-camp inmates are disinfected by an Allied soldier in 1945. Though millions died, thousands lived to testify to Nazi atrocities.

To compound the tragedy, Jewish prisoners often were forced to move the bodies from one point to another. The death toll among Jews alone eventually reached an estimated six million.

German soldiers weren't the only ones to blame for atrocities committed against Jews and other minorities. German public and private records, of which there were tons, show that many civilian business people helped develop ever larger and more efficient means of killing prisoners, all in the name of the Third Reich, the Nazi Party, and Adolf Hitler. These same people, and others, worked to death thousands of prisoners of war and civilian captives who were fed and clothed just enough so they could still produce weapons, ammunition, and supplies for the army. Factories for fuses and other devices were built next to some concentration camps. At one time during the war there were an estimated seven million slave laborers in Germany.

The Third Reich's evil knew no bounds. At a secret meeting in Munich, Germany, in 1942, Nazi physicians devised special diets that would slowly starve to death helpless patients who were extremely ill physically or mentally. A doctor at the conference bragged that, to aid the war effort, he had once grabbed a slice of bread away from a nurse who attempted

to feed a mentally ill patient. These people justified their actions by calling themselves experts in euthanasia — easy or painless death. But death by starvation is neither easy nor painless.

Many of these same physicians subjected foreign civilians and war prisoners — particularly Jews, Gypsies, and Slavs — to hideous experiments. Males were bombarded with x-rays or drugged to make them sterile, and females were forced to undergo operations with the same outcome. Other experiments involved sealing up a prisoner in a chamber and then studying the prisoner's vital signs as the air inside the chamber got gradually thinner, simulating very high altitude, and the prisoner's heart and lungs eventually gave out. The few German civilians and clergy who protested such torture were imprisoned, and at least two teenage German boys were executed for spreading anti-Nazi propaganda.

Rationing and Other Home Front Hardships

For most Americans, particularly minorities and poor people, life was also filled with hardships and injustices. But while life on the home front was made harsher by the war, for many it was more inconvenient than brutal, particularly when compared to what was happening in Europe.

Rationing, which limited how much people could consume, was governed by annoying little books filled with stamps. These 190 million booklets were used eventually to control the purchase of sugar, coffee, cheese, meat, cooking oil, shoes, gasoline, rubber, and other consumables. Gasoline was restricted to three gallons a week, not because the U.S. could not produce enough for domestic use, but because the Japanese held much of the

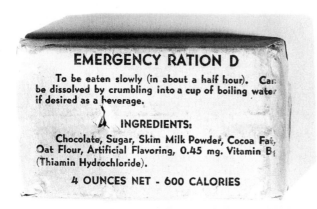

EMERGENCY RATION D

To be eaten slowly (in about a half hour). Can be dissolved by crumbling into a cup of boiling water if desired as a beverage.

INGREDIENTS:

Chocolate, Sugar, Skim Milk Powder, Cocoa Fat, Oat Flour, Artificial Flavoring, 0.45 mg. Vitamin B (Thiamin Hydrochloride).

4 OUNCES NET - 600 CALORIES

Above: This chocolate bar probably was carried by a pilot in case he was forced to ditch his plane and survive in enemy territory.

Right: A grocer points out the value of a rationed product to a consumer, who must pay for the product and give the grocer ration stamps that prevented hoarding.

world's raw rubber supply, which was used to make vehicle tires that would be difficult to replace.

Items that weren't rationed could be scarce. U.S. distilleries ceased making whiskey and other intoxicants and produced whatever kinds of chemicals the government needed. Clothing made of cotton was hard to find because much of the domestic crop was used to make military uniforms. Books, magazines, and newspapers were printed on cheap paper that required fewer chemicals to make. To stabilize the country, other enforced hardships, such as wage and price controls, were shared by everyone. Control of retail prices helped maintain worker morale by helping to assure stable company profits and employee income.

As usual, Americans concentrated on things that took their minds off their problems. Movies were extremely popular, if somewhat predictable, with brave and handsome American soldiers, sailors, and airmen, stereotypically cunning Japanese, and robotic Germans. The women covered a range of types; some wore their country's uniform and others tended to their families and jobs on the home front as they waited for their servicemen sweethearts. The G.I. heroes of these films were fair-haired All-American boys whose best Army buddies invariably were big-city Italian- or Eastern European-Americans who spoke with thick Brooklyn accents.

Women in large numbers gave up trying to find nylon hose and (especially those who went to work in factories) began wearing slacks, while women of Japanese descent, held in detention, put aside for good the traditional kimono. All Americans hummed the same tunes, which often moved to a Latin beat. South American rhythm had invaded the United States in a big way, along with dances demonstrated in the movies by a Brazilian singer with fruit hanging on her hat by the name of Carmen Miranda.

Of course, catchy Latin music was not the only popular music of the day. There were many domestic songs at the time, including such war-related hits as "We're Gonna Find a Feller Who Is Yeller and Beat Him Red, White and Blue." Oddly enough, the most popular song of the war may have been a Bing Crosby tune, "White Christmas." Crosby sang the memorable lyrics in a 1942 movie, *Holiday Inn*. G.I.s and civilians alike got lumps in their throats when "Der Bingle," as German troops fondly called him, oozed out the moving melody. Two or three more Christmases — and countless hardships — would go by before the troops could sing the song at home.

Carmen Miranda, "the Brazilian Bombshell," was one of many entertainers who benefited from the widespread popularity of Latin music in the 1940s. Miranda starred in several motion pictures, dancing and singing in Portuguese beneath ornate costumes.

A flaming Japanese kamikaze aircraft hurtles toward a U.S. Navy aircraft carrier during action near the end of the war. Suicide pilots were recruited after the Japanese navy suffered a series of defeats.

CHAPTER FIVE

The Tide Turns

The largest invasion force ever assembled departed Britain before midnight on June 5, 1944. One thousand ships filled with men and weapons slid away from the white cliffs of Dover and set sail for the French beaches of Normandy. Meanwhile, thousands of British and U.S. paratroopers were climbing aboard airplanes and gliders prior to being dropped behind enemy lines in the middle of the night. D-Day — the "designated day" of the Allied invasion to take Europe back from Nazi Germany — was about to begin.

The Allies had prepared for months, amassing men and military might in England and "softening up" German defenses by bombing airfields and radar stations along the coast of France. And although the Nazis expected the Allies to invade, they did not realize until it was too late that the invasion was underway. It wasn't easy — infantry personnel landing at beaches designated Omaha and Utah and other colorful names were met with barbed wire, ship-piercing barriers hidden in deeper water, and withering fire from sizable, experienced Nazi forces. As dawn broke, increasing numbers of lifeless soldiers bobbed in the tide. But with the help of murderous fire from U.S. and British naval guns, the soldiers fought their way up the cliffs and began to shove the Germans back. They did it with courage, training, and tons of equipment, most of it made in the U.S.

Production Above All

The best soldiers often turn out to be those carrying the best equipment. American production of quality military equipment had an immense impact on the war, since U.S. industry outproduced all the combined enemy's industry. In 1942, for example, the U.S. built forty-six thousand military aircraft. The following year, the total was eighty-six thousand, and the year after that, ninety-six thousand. More than five thousand military oceangoing vessels were constructed, including the Liberty ship, an ugly but efficient cargo vessel. By war's end, a new Liberty ship could be constructed in forty-two days. Henry J. Kaiser's Oakland, California, shipyard once built a Liberty ship in four days! It's no wonder that the average U.S. work week from 1940 to 1944 climbed from 37.7 hours to 46.6 hours.

Manufacturers found themselves building new and unfamiliar objects. Detroit's automakers, even before Pearl Harbor, were assembling aircraft engines for planes being sent to Britain. Tractor factories such as J. I. Case in Racine, Wisconsin, constructed huge transport aircraft. The workforce was made up of men who failed the military's physical examination, as well as older men and women. Smaller manufacturers produced whatever they could sell — a novelty company in Chicago made little artificial flowers out of war stamps that consumers were proud to wear in their buttonholes.

New York City kids collect cans for scrap during World War II. Throughout the nation's metal-saving campaign, aluminum and tin piled up on courthouse lawns all over the country.

Shortages existed in industry and in private life. Metals such as aluminum were always in short supply, though a nationwide scrap drive to turn in aluminum resulted in pots and pans stacked on courthouse lawns and not hauled away for months! Earlier, many of those same courthouses had donated their ornamental cannons during a nationwide drive for iron and steel. In other kinds of drives, people spent their spare time socializing in gymnasiums or churches as they bought or sold bonds or packaged bandages that might save a serviceman's life.

The Black man on the ground has just been punched by several white men as a Detroit police officer separates the combatants. Black-white confrontations took place in many cities as housing shortages pushed the races together.

For unknown reasons, there were sudden, brief shortages of foods such as onions or butter. People were eager and looking for work, and civilians faced housing shortages wherever industry became suddenly busy. Rooming houses often slept three persons to a bed, with each person allowed eight hours in bed out of twenty-four. The other sixteen hours of the day were spent at work or away from the room, which was then occupied by two other workers in turn. Since there were no housing-discrimination laws on the books, owners were free to turn a prospective renter away based on race or ethnic origin, and minorities had a hard time finding living quarters.

Black vs. White Racial Tension

Nowhere was the need for and lack of housing during the war more acute than in Detroit, a city where two million African-Americans moved after Pearl Harbor. Most of them were dirt-poor sharecroppers attracted by the money workers could earn in defense plants. Also lured north were thousands of whites from Appalachia, as poor, as ill-educated, and as hungry as their Black fellow workers. These defense-plant employees and their frequently large families caused the demand for housing to skyrocket. One answer was public housing, an overcrowded, low-cost solution that proved less than ideal.

A disagreement between a Black man and a white man at Detroit's Sojourner Truth housing project started a riot one boiling-hot Sunday in July 1943. The fighting spread from the project to nearby streets and alleys. Fists were replaced by clubs and pipes, and a city policeman was beaten, disarmed, and shot with his own revolver. Fighting continued in large sections of the

city throughout the night and the next day. Michigan's governor asked for and received the aid of federal troops, who calmed matters by affixing bayonets to their rifles. Two dozen Blacks and nine whites died and hundreds were injured. Such showdowns took place frequently during the war years.

Another area important to the war, the port of Beaumont, Texas, was hit by rioting in 1943. A Black shipyard worker was accused of raping a white woman. By the time the authorities proved there was no assault, the town had seen several days of riots followed by martial law. In the East Coast shipyard of Chester, Pennsylvania, near Philadelphia, white guards shot five Black demonstrators protesting discrimination in hiring policies. Disruptions also took place at defense plants in Massachusetts and Ohio.

The year 1943 would be remembered by residents of New York City for the eruption that took place in Harlem. Like the conflict in Detroit, this unrest was caused by substandard living conditions and high rents charged by landlords who were taking advantage of the huge demand for places to live. The problem was compounded by charges of police brutality, a credible statement in view of the fact that the city's police were overwhelmingly white. Five New Yorkers were killed, more than four hundred were wounded, and the destruction of property amounted to $5 million.

The Zoot Suit Riots and Other Conflicts at Home

Los Angeles saw a different kind of problem. Young people, primarily Mexican-American teenage boys, began to dress in zoot suits. These suits had been introduced by African-American entertainer Cab Calloway and consisted of very long coats with padded shoulders, baggy pants pegged tightly at the ankle, dress hats with feathers, and long watch chains that almost dragged to the ground. Annoying to parents, other residents, and the authorities, unemployed and undereducated zoot suiters hung out aimlessly on street corners (with their girlfriends, who wore shiny "juke jackets") while everyone else went to school, to jobs, or to the military.

Above: A Black-owned car is tipped over by a gang of whites in Detroit. The military had to be called in to break up the July 1943 riots.

Below: Zoot suits were worn by Mexican-American boys and men, particularly in Los Angeles, where they often were attacked by military men going to, or returning from, fighting in the Pacific.

Southern California was filled with military people on their way to or from the war, and soldiers and sailors clashed savagely and frequently with the teenagers. There were so many fights that the Navy declared all of Los Angeles temporarily off limits. The city council outlawed the wearing of zoot suits, and Los Angeles police enforced the ban with occasional brutality. Police consistently defended the soldiers and sailors, who were in the habit of picking fights with Mexican-Americans and other minorities.

More dangerous, if less flamboyant, than the zoot suiters were the tiny number of right-wing extremists and racists who blamed the war on its most obvious Jewish victims, or took their frustrations out on Blacks, the country's most slighted minority. Militant anti-Semites, race baiters, uniformed Nazis, and other people with hateful agendas were brought in a group to federal trial on charges of sedition in 1944. These peddlers of hate literature and fans of fascism were kept occupied during the trial's six months of harangues, charges, countercharges, and delays, all of which resulted in a mistrial after the judge fell over dead.

All such unrest had a few positive results. Civic leaders from many different areas gathered in large and small cities to try to improve matters. The most successful effort was the American Council on Race Relations, begun in Chicago. Many meetings were led by priests and ministers and by the National Association for the Advancement of Colored People (NAACP). These people worked at making the last two war years, 1944 and 1945, peaceful ones, at least at home.

Some cities, in fact, were much more affected by war than others. Inland, industrial cities such as Cincinnati noticed how much better the economy had suddenly become. Because many precision machines were made in the city, and because men were being drafted constantly, there was as much work as anyone could handle. On the coasts, things were even busier. San Francisco oozed urgency as soldiers and sailors prepared to go or returned from overseas. Later in the conflict, people living around San Francisco Bay were often reminded of war's horror. They watched as huge aircraft carriers and other U.S. Navy ships, twisted from hits by Japanese *kamikaze* ("divine wind") suicide planes, limped under the Golden Gate Bridge into nearby Oakland's shipyards for repairs. But at least they were working — despite the horrors of war, a welcome development after the long Depression.

War Heroes

All countries have their heroes, and the U.S. in World War II was no different. Most U.S. heroes were small-town white males, because America at the time still had many small towns and white males greatly outnumbered U.S. soldiers of all other kinds. Such a hero was Richard Bong, from a farm outside Poplar, Wisconsin, a tiny village near the chilly shores of Lake Superior. Bong was America's aerial ace in World War II, shooting down more planes — forty — than any U.S. pilot before or since. Sent to the Pacific, he and his P-38 fighter gunned down as many as five Japanese planes in a single battle, earning for Bong the Congressional Medal of Honor. Yet this son of a Swedish immigrant did not outlive the war. He was killed on August 6, 1945, in California while testing a new jet plane.

Ethnic minorities were well represented among the ranks of war heroes throughout World War II. U.S. Marine Mitchell Page, a native of Yugoslavia who was born Milan Pejic, won the Medal of Honor on Guadalcanal in the vicious and drawn-out jungle fighting that took place there. Fellow Slav Peter Tomich died earlier in the war, at Pearl Harbor. This Medal of Honor winner stayed at his weapon aboard the U.S.S. *Utah*, covering his shipmates until he was gunned down by a Japanese plane. Slovenian native and U.S. Navy Lieutenant Commander Milton Pavlic sank three ships and shot down thirty-two planes before dying in battle aboard the U.S.S. *Dakota* in the Pacific.

An African-American man, Dorie Miller, distinguished himself even before war was declared. Working as a U.S. Navy mess (kitchen) attendant, Miller leaped to an antiaircraft gun at Pearl Harbor and brought down an attacking Japanese plane. His courage under fire had far-reaching results: the Navy examined its policy toward African-Americans and saw to it that fifty-eight Black men eventually were made officers. The Marines, really part of the Navy, also used African-Americans in combat roles, while the U.S. Coast Guard commissioned seven hundred Black officers and ended up

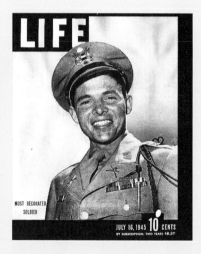

America's most-decorated soldier

Only 433 people received the Medal of Honor in World War II. Of those, just 190 survived the brave deeds that earned them the medal. Among the survivors was a slight, baby-faced young man from Texas named Audie L. Murphy.

One of twelve children, Murphy was so poor that he had attended only five years of school in his first fifteen years. He attempted to enlist in the Army but was initially thought too small. Filling himself with food and carrying a note from a sister that proved he was indeed eighteen, the Texan joined the U.S. Army infantry.

Murphy was sent to North Africa but saw his first action in Sicily. He was wounded there before rejoining his unit for the drive through Italy. After that, Murphy and fellow infantrymen went to France. They arrived shortly after D-Day and joined the pursuit of Germans eastward. On January 26, 1945, the recently promoted Lieutenant Murphy and eighteen fellow soldiers were holding a patch of woods when they were attacked by two hundred German foot soldiers backed up by six tanks.

The Americans had only two vehicles with enough firepower to destroy a tank, and one of them was knocked out by a blast from an enemy cannon. Ordering his men to retreat, Murphy climbed atop the damaged vehicle and began firing a machine gun as he called in artillery fire. Hidden by smoke and exploding shells, Murphy shot dozens of Germans while the artillery disabled the tanks. He had turned back a small army all by himself.

Murphy was hailed long and loud on his return. He had won thirty-three medals, including three Purple Hearts for wounds and the Congressional Medal of Honor. After some success as a movie actor, Murphy began to gamble. While trying in 1971 to recoup his money by becoming a real-estate developer, he was killed in the crash of a light plane.

with four thousand Black recruits — all because of Dorie Miller, who won the Navy Cross for his gallantry under fire.

Among the many moving stories to come out of World War II was one about a Los Angeles resident who loved baseball. The trouble was, Sadao Munemori's parents were Japanese. So he was told by the federal government early in 1942 to put aside his mechanics' tools and his fielder's mitt and report to an inland camp. After only a few weeks at the camp, Munemori escaped the boredom by volunteering for the military. Eventually, he found himself fighting with the Japanese-American 442nd Regimental Combat Team in northern Italy.

While some Japanese-American units were sent to the Pacific, the 442nd was a highly decorated unit sent to Europe rather than to the Japanese-controlled Pacific. In 1944, the 442nd accomplished one of the most dramatic and celebrated missions in the war: the rescue of the "Lost Battalion," three hundred Texans of the 36th Division that had been surrounded by the Nazis for a week. Taking only thirty minutes to break through Nazi lines, the 442nd lost over half its men in the fight. The toast of the entire United States, all members of the 442nd were later made honorary citizens of Texas by proclamation of the governor.

On the day for which he will be remembered, Munemori led members of his unit through a minefield. Using skills picked up on California playgrounds, he then silenced a German machine-gun emplacement by hurling a hand grenade. Another machine gun opened up on the Americans, and Munemori killed those Germans, too, again with a well-placed grenade. As he turned to his buddies waiting in a shell crater, a German hand grenade bounced off Munemori's helmet and landed among his friends. Without hesitation, Munemori threw himself on the grenade and died instantly, thereby saving his comrades. For his actions, he was posthumously awarded the Congressional Medal of Honor.

Above: Dorie Miller receives the Navy Cross for heroism at Pearl Harbor.

Below: The Medal of Honor is pinned on the mother of Sadao Munemori, who hurled himself on a German grenade in Italy to prevent the deaths of his comrades.

Americans loved their heroes but weren't always sure who the cowards were. George Patton, an Army general who led a tank division, thought he knew. Twice during the war, while visiting wounded men in field hospitals, Patton slapped soldiers who showed no outward signs of injury yet were shell shocked — jarred by the concussion of explosions or otherwise stunned. The public grew angry at Patton's lack of sensitivity — was this any way to treat victims of trauma? Furor over the incidents died down, but the abrasive general had to wait a while for his next promotion.

The 1944 Presidential Election
and a Conservative Tilt

Once war news began to turn in the Allies' favor, Republicans gathered strength at home. President Roosevelt had beaten Republican candidate Wendell Willkie in 1940, but the Republicans had a new candidate, a crusading prosecuting attorney by the name of Thomas E. Dewey, and the country was becoming more conservative. Adding to Democratic woes was the health of the president. Roosevelt had been confined to a wheelchair as the result of polio since his thirties, and the effects of the disease plus the weight of public office were beginning to show. He was almost bald, his skin seemed to hang, and he coughed incessantly because of his addiction to cigarettes.

Two things helped keep Roosevelt in the White House. The first was Dewey's stuffy appearance. A fellow Republican, Alice Roosevelt Longworth, said Dewey's thin, carefully trimmed mustache made him look like the groom on a wedding cake! The other was the insistence by rural, southern Democrats and big-city machine Democrats alike that Henry Wallace be dumped as the vice president in favor of a less progressive candidate. The Democratic convention became a tug-of-war between these more conservative forces and the progressives, who liked the mild form of socialism Wallace advocated. In the end, the vice president stepped down and a moderate Democratic U.S. senator from Missouri, Harry S. Truman, took his place. The Roosevelt-Truman ticket won the closest election since the victory of Woodrow Wilson in 1916, another war year.

Henry Wallace did not just fade away. Instead, he crusaded for the things he believed in and ran a third-party campaign as a socialist in 1948. He continued to have the support of intellectuals, some union members, and a significant number of African-American voters. Before stepping down in 1944, he told Democrats what he thought the country needed — elimination of the poll tax so that Blacks and the poor could vote, equal education for all, and equal pay for equal work, regardless of race or sex. Such a message was too progressive for the war years and proved not much more popular in the presidential campaign four years later.

Meanwhile, as U.S. forces were landing in the Leyte Gulf to reclaim the Philippines, the United States' four million aliens were being given careful scrutiny. Several states passed laws that were obviously unconstitutional but stayed on the books for brief periods. In Pennsylvania, for example, only U.S. citizens could possess

Above: President Franklin D. Roosevelt, while still governor of New York. The president lived with the effects of polio as he served the nation from 1932 until his death in 1945.

Below: Harry S. Truman succeeded Roosevelt and made the decision to use atomic weapons on the Japanese.

Above: White actors mockingly portrayed African-Americans in "Amos 'n' Andy."

Below: Paul Robeson won critical acclaim for his portrayal of Shakespeare's Othello.

hunting or fishing licenses. Some states did not permit aliens to own dogs. Pennsylvania and Georgia forced all aliens within their borders to register so that, in any sort of emergency, they could be rounded up. Some of these aliens were trapped in the U.S. by war and didn't want to be on domestic soil any more than Americans wanted them here. The extent of civil-liberties abuses was nowhere near that in Europe, where Jews, Slavs, Gypsies, homosexuals, people with disabilities, and other groups were not only forced to register but deported, tortured, and even exterminated. But the eagerness of the wartime U.S. government to suspend the rights of selected citizens and alien residents provides an uncomfortable foot-note to any history of the nation's noble fight for democracy abroad.

Among the general public, foreigners became the butt of jokes, but no more so than African-Americans, who continued to suffer in the mainstream media. "Amos 'n' Andy," a radio comedy show that featured white men portraying Black men, was immensely popular with the European-American majority. Audiences loved the way characters with names like Kingfish supposedly murdered the English language and fell for preposterous schemes. In a similar vein, *The Saturday Evening Post* began a cartoon called "Ambitious Ambrose." He was an African-American boy who wanted to work hard but could not understand the simplest directions and therefore made supposedly humorous mistakes.

In contrast to these demeaning characters, Hollywood began to portray African-Americans more realistically and sympathetically. Films such as *The Ox-Bow Incident* featured Blacks who acted with intelligence in serious roles. Instead of an all-Black film every three or four years, studios began to produce that many each year by war's end. One such quality production was *In This Our Life*, the story of a chauffeur's struggle to support himself and study law. On Broadway, singer-actor Paul Robeson was im-mensely popular as Shakespeare's Othello. All-Black dramatic productions that were successes included *Carmen Jones* and *Anna Lucasta*. Newspapers and magazines began to more regularly review these and other produc-tions, taking the quality of the performances seriously.

The Veterans Return

Though the war was by no means over, a million veterans were returned to civilian life by the spring of 1944. A full array of benefits awaited those who wanted to take advantage of them, though the benefits were offset by predictions of massive unemployment and by occasional confrontations between vets and civilians. One of the miracles of this period was the transition from a wartime to a peace-time economy without enormous economic upheavals. Firms were required by law to rehire a vet at his old job, but more than 70 percent of returning veterans either used the G.I. Bill to further their educa-tion or found new and better jobs on their own. A housing boom brought on by returning veterans ready to settle down with their new families brought an even rosier bloom to the nation's economy.

If the virtually all-male legions of returning veterans were the winners, women were the losers. At the peak of wartime production near the end of 1943, they had made up one-third of the work force with some seventeen million women employed. But women were bumped out of jobs by returning vets or laid off as the need for wartime materials, and thus their services, declined. The federal government backed equal pay for equal work, but most women realized they had been paid less than men performing the same tasks. Despite unequal and occasional harsh treatment, women had shown they could perform almost any job they were given and perform it well. By war's end, one union member in five was a woman, and women were found in most offices. Modest as this now seems, it was a historic change in female roles.

While women's roles expanded during the war years, children seemed to have been forgotten. Teenagers in particular were too old to participate in door-to-door scrap drives with little red wagons, as their younger brothers and sisters did. And yet they were too young for war and had little to do with their time because transportation was rationed. Many children became latchkey kids as their mothers worked longer hours during wartime production drives. A PTA program set up to protect children during air raids instead uncovered many cases of child neglect and wound up looking after children on a local, voluntary basis.

But if young people endured hardship here, their lot in Germany was even more difficult. British and U.S. bombers overwhelmed German defenses, leveling most major cities. Though the Germans managed to move many of their warmaking factories to rural locations, they could only watch helplessly as their homes — plus huge chemical, steel, and petroleum plants — were blown to bits. Food was sometimes scarce — civilians told of cities with nothing to eat for weeks on end but withered root crops. By the middle of the war, all able-bodied males had been pulled from German colleges into the military.

University of Munich students, who had strongly supported Hitler ten years earlier, called in 1943 for peace in street demonstrations. A brother and sister, Hans and Sophie Scholl, were seen distributing leaflets and were turned in to the secret police by a janitor following a college riot. Both were grilled, tortured, tried, and eventually hanged. While their case was one of the more celebrated of its kind to come out of Nazi Germany, Hans and Sophie Scholl were but two of a number of civilians who tried to end the war in Europe.

English children sleep in makeshift hammocks slung in London's underground railway in 1940. The British rallied with air power to flatten most German cities by the end of the war.

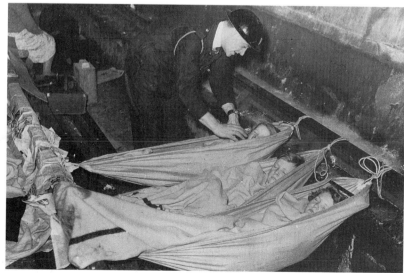

Detonation of an atomic bomb. Note the surplus ships, used to gauge the power of the device, at the base of the explosion. U.S. scientists knew the bomb's power but did not anticipate its long-term effect on humans.

CHAPTER SIX

War's Terrible End

Hitler's generals saw the end coming and tried several times to do away with him. They failed because he kept no regular schedule, arriving before a bomb could be placed or departing before it blew up. (Surrounded as he was by bodyguards, it would have been suicidal to try to shoot him.) A supposedly foolproof bomb was put on his plane one night as it left the Eastern Front. The British-made weapon failed to detonate, and a nervous general had to quietly retrieve it later. One assassination attempt, perhaps the most nearly successful and certainly one of the most publicized, cost several lives, including that of Hitler's favorite and most successful general, Field Marshal Erwin Rommel.

The Desert Fox, as Rommel was known, was put in charge of troops that were to hold back the Allies following the invasion of Europe. On June 5, 1944 — the day before D-Day, the date of the Allied invasion — the general decided to drive from France to Germany for a meeting. He was unable to fly because Allied planes controlled the skies along the coast of France, and Hitler did not want to risk the lives of his generals. Rommel conducted military affairs in Germany, learned with surprise of the Normandy invasion, and returned to France. He was driving in Normandy on July 17 when his car was shot up by an Allied fighter plane. Rommel's injuries included shrapnel wounds and a skull fracture. Doctors feared for his life.

So did army officers in Germany who had looked to him for strength in a plot to kill Hitler. Rommel and several fellow officers who loved Germany hated the destruction of their cities by Allied air power. They believed that Hitler, with his constant orders never to retreat or regroup, was wiping out both the nation and the military. The Allied invasion distracted the plotters, but they did rig a time bomb, and it was planted in a brief case during a meeting with the Führer on July 20, 1944, by a one-armed, one-eyed veteran, a young colonel named Von Stauffenberg. The bomb exploded, but it had been placed against a leg of the table, and thanks to the heavy table top, it only injured Hitler. It did kill three others.

Revenge was swift. The plotters were rounded up, questioned, tortured, and executed. In some cases, their families were sent to concentration camps

General Erwin Rommel, Hitler's most successful general, inspects sea-wall defenses shortly before D-Day, 1944. Rommel was involved in the plot to kill Hitler and committed suicide rather than stand trial.

without trials. Even people who had merely mentioned getting rid of Hitler were themselves punished or killed. A total of seven thousand arrests in connection with the bombing were made by the secret police, and almost five thousand people in all were executed. Because Rommel was not present, and because he had served his country well, he was asked if he wanted to quietly take poison. He accepted and was given a state funeral; the public was told that the Desert Fox had died of his earlier injuries.

One reason that high-ranking officers laid their lives on the line to get rid of Hitler was that Germany was taking a bashing in the war. By the midpoint in the war, Allied planes outnumbered and therefore outgunned the Luftwaffe. While antiaircraft ground fire could be thick and deadly, it could only do so much against wave after wave of U.S. and British bombers. The British harbored special reasons for laying waste to Germany: their own cities, from London in the south to Coventry in the Midlands, had been hammered by German bombs early in the war. By war's end, much of Europe would lie in ruins.

A Beaten Enemy?

Meanwhile, on the Western Front, the fighting in 1944 was vicious from town to town throughout France. The constant warfare led American G.I.s to wonder how long it would be before they were injured or killed. Adding to the discomfort was the winter weather, with its freezing temperatures, sullen skies, and frequent snows. Things didn't get any better as the U.S. Army spearhead surged eastward, in the direction of Belgium and Germany. Withdrawing Nazi soldiers left snipers in the trees securely tied to large branches in otherwise precarious positions. U.S. soldiers moving beneath them were shot in the back before their comrades could kill the enemy tied to the large chestnut or oak tree limb.

The G.I.s who had somehow survived fighting from D-Day on began to notice a change in the German troops. They were as determined as ever, but there were several subtle differences. Their clothing seldom fit — it was often too small but more often too large. It was dirty and torn and stuffed with bits of blanket to ward off the snowy weather. The soldiers carried hardly any spare ammunition, and they seemed either very young or very old. Could Germany be running out of military-age males with which to carry on a war it had started five years before?

Able-bodied German soldiers remained, but Hitler was holding them back so that he could spring a trap on the Allies. Aware of the effects of winter weather, which had helped defeat the Germans at Stalingrad, Hitler planned a surprise lunge westward through Belgium in December 1944. Germany had charged through the heavily forested area in 1940 when the army had bypassed the fortified French line to overrun Belgium and roar into France. This time, he hoped to break the morale, if not the back, of the U.S., British,

French, and other forces with a huge attack that would cut the enemy in two. With the Soviets momentarily stalled in the east, Hitler summoned his generals and explained his plan.

The Battle of the Bulge

The final German offensive of the war began shortly before Christmas in 1944. The Führer rounded up every German soldier, tank, artillery piece, aircraft, and supply truck in existence and hurled it at the onrushing Allies in the hilly forests of Belgium. The Nazis attacked along a seventy-mile front, taking advantage of stormy weather, which kept U.S. and British planes on the ground. Within two days, the Nazis were within a few miles of U.S. First Army headquarters, which was quickly evacuated. The resistance was ragged, but it did slow the German drive near the small Belgian town of Bastogne.

The few First Army soldiers in Bastogne became more optimistic when the U.S. 101st Airborne Division was rushed in to reinforce them. Yet they remained vastly outnumbered and outgunned. The airborne division's commanding general, A. C. McAuliffe, was asked on December 22 if he and his men intended to give up. The general gave the Germans a one-word answer: "Nuts!" Though people in the United States did not hear about McAuliffe's terse reply until after the 101st had successfully put up the fight of its life, the veteran soldier became an instant hit with the folks back home.

Several things then fell into place for the Americans, but not before the German offensive had cost the U.S. an astonishing fifty-five thousand dead and eighteen thousand captured. The skies cleared, and air power pounded German armored units. General Patton and his own armored division showed up and added their muscle to the fight. The Germans could not count on a constant supply of fuel and frequently had to wait for sluggish supplies to catch up to them. Despite later counterattacks, the Battle of the Bulge — the Nazi lunge into Belgium designed to protect Germany — failed.

Blacks to the Front

As the war in Europe wound down, more and more African-Americans saw frontline fighting. Among the very best outfits was an all-Black unit — the 761st Tank Battalion, also known as the Black Panthers — that had chafed for action all through training and attacked the Germans with a vengeance once they set foot in Europe. This group of tankers, shrugging off the grim statistic that a tank has a life of about ten minutes in a battle, helped liberate German concentration camps. For years after the war's end, Jewish survivors recalled the magnificent sight of these soldiers and their tanks crashing through the gates at Buchenwald and other camps. For some, it was the first time they had seen Black soldiers, and for them these G.I.s — victims of racial injustice in their own segregated Army — were like angels from heaven.

About 700,000 African-American soldiers served in World War II. Some 160,000 passed through Britain, usually on their way to continental Europe.

U.S. troops guard captured German SS troops as the Battle of the Bulge fails in Belgium early in 1945. The German offensive caught the Allies by surprise but was eventually subdued with armor and air power.

French troops share candy with Black American forces after fighting side by side in Germany in 1945.

They were segregated from whites in the Army in preparation for D-Day. With a few exceptions, all of the senior officers leading Black units were white males. Commanding officers could be good, bad, and in-between, and like some judges at home in the U.S., many of these officers were often biased in handing out justice among the troops.

Desertions by whites and Blacks alike increased as the war went on. In the frightening explosions, noise, and smoke of battle, it was easy to slip away from the action. By the time the Allies were well into France, soldiers were increasingly edgy and sometimes tried to hide in villages freshly captured from the Nazis. France had several African colonies at the time and was more racially tolerant than the U.S., and the average French citizen, having lived five years under the German boot, was eager to see an American of any color. Though food was scarce, more than one American was fed and offered shelter by grateful farm and village families. It was the closest thing some soldiers came to time off, though the U.S. rotated soldiers into and out of battles every few days.

If being a white soldier was difficult with the end of the war in sight, it was twice as tough being Black. For much of the conflict, the white majority had implied that Blacks didn't have what it took — intelligence, courage, whatever — to be good frontline troops. Consequently, Black men had to prove themselves first as fellow humans, then as skilled fighters to the skeptical military. One large group of African-Americans that succeeded in this double effort was the U.S. Army's all-Black 92nd Division.

Buffalo Soldiers

The 92nd Division came to life at remote Fort Huachuca, Arizona, probably the only place large enough to train an entire division of African-Americans without their mixing with European-Americans! These soldiers were commanded by Major General Edward M. Almond, who was from Virginia. Like most of his senior officers, Almond was white. Blacks filled in the ranks of junior officers (lieutenants and captains) and enlisted personnel (privates, corporals, various grades of sergeant). The 92nd totaled fifteen thousand men and was nicknamed the Buffalo Division for the "buffalo soldiers" (Black cavalry members) who helped tame the West in the nineteenth century. Before leaving Arizona, they were given a buffalo as a mascot, which they promptly named Bill!

Many of the men of the 92nd grew impatient for action. They were sent to Italy in the spring of 1944, and by June found themselves headed northward and locked in combat with German forces. Because any Black Army member seen as a troublemaker was shipped to the 92nd, the relationship between white officers and some of the Blacks became strained. Yet the division as a whole received about the same number of awards and decorations as others fighting at the time. A total of 515 members were killed in action and 2,242 were wounded.

Another division of Black soldiers, the 93rd, fought in the Pacific. An unfortunate incident in 1944 marred the 93rd's record and backed claims of white people that "Negro" soldiers were cowardly in battle. A small unit from the 93rd, all inexperienced soldiers, hid in caves after being fired upon by a Japanese force they outnumbered on the island of Bougainville in the Solomon chain. This story was blown out of proportion until the tale was told that the entire division had fallen apart on hearing enemy gunfire. Whites who told the story apparently had forgotten — or ignored — the fact that an even larger force of white soldiers had run after meeting Afrika Korps Germans at the Battle of Kasserine Pass in 1943.

Casualties Continue

Neither the Germans nor the Japanese rolled over and played dead for anyone. In the Pacific, the battle for Okinawa produced fifty thousand U.S. casualties, all for an island only four hundred square miles in size. Some seven million Japanese army members and militia personnel were digging in to protect their homeland from the oncoming Americans. And although Americans and Soviets were closing in on Berlin, the ill-equipped Germans refused to surrender. By the spring of 1945, with Churchill, Stalin, and Roosevelt meeting at Yalta in the Soviet Union to think about the postwar world, two events took place that would shove other news off the front page.

President Roosevelt went to Warm Springs, a Georgia resort, for a rest. Complaining of a headache, he lay down on April 12 and died in his sleep of a brain hemorrhage. Many of those who loved him wept uncontrollably, and

The death of Private Slovik

For a soldier, the only thing worse than being killed in war is being the last person to die. After the successful landing by Allied forces on the beaches of France on D-Day, everyone knew that the war was coming to an end. Consequently, desertions occurred in increasing numbers as the Allies pushed the Germans out of France. The only soldier in World War II who deserted and paid with his life was Private Eddie Slovik.

Slovik was a married ex-convict who arrived in France in 1944. In the face of his first enemy artillery barrage, Slovik hid. The following day, he turned himself in to Canadian forces, who handed him over to U.S. troops several weeks later. He deserted again before turning himself in again and writing a statement that he would desert once more in the face of a barrage of artillery.

Slovik was found guilty of desertion on November 11, 1944, in a trial that lasted only one hundred minutes. There were no appeals allowed, so he was placed against a garden wall near Elbeuf, France, and shot to death on January 31, 1945. Slovik's death is important because he was held to a different standard than the many other deserters at the time. Of 2,864 Army personnel tried for the crime of desertion, 49 were sentenced to death. But only Eddie Slovik was executed — perhaps, some say, as an example to other would-be deserters as the war came to an end.

Slovik was no angel; he was convicted of car theft in Michigan before being drafted and had spent time in prison. Did his civilian record influence the six officers who handed down his sentence? The officers say it did not. A few years after the execution, a right-wing group claimed President Roosevelt had ordered Slovik's death because he was Catholic! For years after the war, the entire matter continued to fascinate Americans. Martin Sheen played the deserter in a popular made-for-television movie produced in 1974.

even those who disliked him realized that he had successfully led the United States through a terrible time. Less than a month later, on May 7, Germany surrendered as U.S. and Soviet troops met amid the rubble that once was the Third Reich. Hitler, his wife, and several aides and their families committed suicide rather than be taken by either side. Almost immediately, Americans began to wonder if a capitalist state like the U.S. would get along with a communist state such as the U.S.S.R.

U.S. soldiers never saw most of the German death camps. The camps were in Poland and other areas east of Germany that three years of war had put back in the hands of Soviet troops. But they did liberate and see for themselves several of the older and larger camps, stacked high with bony corpses and dusty with the ashes of the dead. Auschwitz, today the scene of a Holocaust museum, saw 6,000-16,000 deaths every day for weeks and months. Miraculously, a few prisoners were alive when U.S. forces arrived. These wasted, helpless people really were the most fit among all prisoners, since they had somehow survived for months or even years with scraps of food and endless slave labor.

Again, meticulous Nazi records show just how terrible things actually were. According to their logs and diaries, the people in charge of the camps searched constantly for new and speedier ways to rid the earth of Germany's foes. Buildings that appeared to be innocent showers or delousing facilities were in reality gas chambers. Intensely poisonous gas crystals such as Zyklon-B were used in Auschwitz at the rate of several tons a month. Between slave labor and extinction, approximately eleven million Jews, Slavs, Gypsies, and enemies of the state were doomed.

Germans didn't abide by the customary rules of armed conflict when it came to handling prisoners of war. Thousands of Poles and Soviets were killed in eastern Poland in a remote area known as Babi Yar. Other military and political officers were killed immediately when they were captured. Remains discovered for years after the war added evidence to what was already known —that the Nazis had exterminated many of their captives. The Germans also killed about seventy British pilots, prisoners of war who were tortured or shot after they were caught trying to escape. In the Battle of the Bulge, several dozen captured Americans were lined up and shot with automatic weapons.

The Japanese treated prisoners of war little better than the Germans. Their culture dictated that military people should always fight to the end, so they showed only contempt for prisoners of war. Many were decapitated or bayoneted or worked to death in intense tropical climates. Civilians and native guerrilla fighters were treated at least as badly, the Filipino people being mowed down almost at will by Japanese soldiers. Captured British, Indian, Burmese, and Malay soldiers were forced to build roads and railroads through dense jungle using little more than their bare hands.

The war's victors weren't always entirely humane, either. Captured Germans held in France under the command of General Dwight D. Eisenhower were systematically starved. The number of dead may have run into the hundreds or even thousands. And the Soviets killed a large but unknown number of Germans. On all fronts and in the case of virtually all participating nations, this World War II pushed the killing of human beings to new and terrible heights as agreements on the conduct of war became meaningless in the face of new and terrible weapons.

Dropping the Atomic Bomb

The U.S. Navy cruiser *Indianapolis* was torpedoed only four days after it left the first atomic bomb on the island of Tinian, east of the Philippines. The bomb was fourteen feet long and weighed ten thousand pounds. It was carefully loaded aboard a four-engine B-29 bomber, nicknamed *Enola Gay*, during the predawn hours of August 6, 1945. The big bomber roared down the runway and into the Pacific darkness at 2:45 A.M.

On board, besides the nine-man crew, were three people who knew how to make the bomb work. They set about activating it; readying it took just twenty-five minutes. The first hint of dawn appeared after 4:00 A.M., before the *Enola Gay* passed over the island of Iwo Jima and began radio silence. Two other B-29s were involved in the flight, for film and observation purposes. The pilots were told to bring back still and motion-picture film but not to fly through the cloud the bomb would produce.

Hiroshima, a large, southern industrial city, was ringed with clouds but the sky was fairly clear, as it was over the second- and third-choice targets. The bomb was dropped at 8:16 A.M. and was set to go off at 1,850 feet above ground for maximum effect. It exploded as intended, sending a blinding yellow-white flash of light that quickly caught up with the planes and the crews, who were wearing heavy welding goggles as a precaution. There followed two waves of explosions, traveling an estimated twelve miles a minute, one from the bomb and one rebounding off the ground. "My God," said one crew member. "What have we done?"

Among the things they did was to burn the flesh off of living human beings in a radius of two and one-half miles. Of more than three hundred thousand residents, one hundred thousand died and another one hundred thousand were injured. Also killed were U.S. and Dutch prisoners of war being held in the industrial city. One of the trailing B-29s believed the *Enola Gay* had missed

Crew members of the *Enola Gay*, the B-29 bomber that dropped the atomic bomb on Hiroshima on August 6, 1945.

its target because there was nothing on the ground below that resembled a city. Not even the worst previous fire bombings wiped out traces of city blocks and roads, yet this new bomb had evaporated all evidence of humankind in a city the size of present-day Buffalo, New York.

Japanese who were living or stationed in Germany when the Nazis fell from power had approached Americans about ending the war in the spring of 1945. But the Japanese military did not want to surrender. The Japanese government's first indication of the kind of weapon

Only rubble remains in Nagasaki, the second Japanese city hit with an atomic weapon. The bomb was dropped far from the city's center but caused horrific damage and loss of life.

to be used against them came from former students who had gone to college in the U.S. and were employed to monitor American radio broadcasts. They told their superiors about talk of an atomic bomb, how it had the power of twenty thousand tons of TNT, and how its use would prevent the need for a U.S. invasion on one of the main Japanese islands, Kyushu.

The second bomb, dropped three days later on Nagasaki, was equally devastating. A plutonium device, it also created heat at its center of 100 million degrees, though the bombardier who dropped it missed his target by three miles. This bomb could not be activated in the air, and the B-29 nicknamed *Bock's Car* took off from Tinian with the explosive device ready to detonate. After this second thunderous explosion and the tremendous destruction and loss of life it brought to this city of 250,000, the Japanese asked for clarification of U.S. terms of surrender and then gave up on August 14, 1945.

What Can Be Learned?

Did the United States have to use the atomic bomb? That question has been asked ever since the terrible destructive power of the device was widely known. There remains no definite answer, though clues are strewn across the map of the U.S., the Pacific Ocean, Japan, and beyond.

Military people believe dropping the bomb was necessary because the Japanese were prepared to fight to the death. The bomb, these soldiers claim, actually saved the lives of many Japanese, as well as countless thousands of U.S. soldiers. They remind us that the Americans were preparing in August of 1945 to invade Japan's main islands. They further point to mass suicides of civilians in places such as Okinawa after the Japanese military had convinced them that an American conquest would be brutal and cruel. General MacArthur believed that Japanese civilians could practice guerrilla warfare for ten years.

The decision became complicated when the presidency was passed from Roosevelt to Truman. Since a single atomic bomb had the power of twenty thousand tons of TNT, why didn't the U.S. provide a demonstration of its power? The flaw here, advisors report, is that the device might not have worked. And if it had failed, Japan would have resisted all the harder. Yet another option, a U.S. Navy blockade of Japan, could have taken years and, critics argue, might have resulted in more deaths than the bombs. Truman's decision was clouded by the fact that he learned very late of the Manhattan Project — the $2 billion race to build the first bomb. To greatly simplify matters, would he launch the Big Invasion or drop the Big Bomb? He chose the latter.

Other factors in the dropping of the bomb had less to do with military strategy. Primarily, scientists did not understand radiation or know that it would damage so many human beings. Most of those who worked on the Manhattan Project were shocked at the death and disfigurement from the fallout that followed the explosion. Both the uranium bomb that fell on Hiroshima and the plutonium bomb dropped over Nagasaki caused hideous, widespread injury that will affect the genes of the survivors for generations. As someone remarked, the lucky victims died.

The Cost of War

Although the United States emerged from World War II the strongest nation on earth, the outcome didn't necessarily prove to be "good" for the victor. The U.S. lost 292,131 members of the military, people who might have contributed to the country's well-being in even better ways, had they been given a chance as civilians. More than 16.3 million U.S. adults spent time in the armed forces, preventing them from performing more productive and meaningful work at home. Worldwide, deaths totaled one million a month for more months than anyone cared to count.

Soldiers from Java (part of Indonesia), held prisoner by the Japanese in Nagasaki, show burns they suffered in the atomic blast. Note how clothing the men wore protected them from burns, seen on exposed areas such as faces and necks. The man in the middle was burned on his legs because he was wearing shorts.

At least forty-six million people worldwide lost their lives in World War II. That is as many people as currently reside in the states of Alabama, Alaska, Arizona, Arkansas, California, Colorado, and Connecticut combined. Looked at another way, the deaths exceed the combined populations of modern-day Australia and Canada.

Who were these people? In addition to military personnel, many were innocent civilians, including children, who were caught in the crossfire; many others were equally innocent civilians branded as enemies of the Axis governments to be despised and targeted for genocide. What scientific or humanitarian breakthroughs might people from these groups have made if they had lived out their lives?

Jews. Almost six million Jews, about two-thirds of the Jewish population of prewar Europe, were murdered by the Nazis and their collaborators. Anti-Semitism was a cornerstone of the twisted Nazi view of what life on earth should be like. Jews had been blamed down through history for everything from crop failures to widespread illness to the crucifixion of Christ. The Nazis convinced many fellow Germans that the Jewish minority had somehow betrayed Germany during World War I and that this sellout caused social unrest and economic depression. Jews were restricted, then imprisoned, then herded together and killed. Jews in occupied lands such as Poland, the Ukraine, Russia, Hungary, Romania, Yugoslavia, France, the Netherlands, and elsewhere were deported, to be murdered by the hundreds of thousands.

Gypsies. One-third of Europe's Gypsy population, or three hundred thousand Gypsies in all, were put to death. The only thing that saved many of them was their mobility. Most were nomads, moving frequently from town to town. So when fascist forces advanced toward them, the Gypsies fled or hid

European Gypsies. These nomadic people trace their lineage to ancient India. They were considered racially inferior by the Nazis and were imprisoned or killed.

These French soldiers, from Senegal in West Africa, escaped a German labor gang and were hidden by the French underground resistance until liberation in August 1944. Here, they pose with a member of the underground.

their families and wagons in thick forests. On the other hand, their dark complexions and colorful clothing made them easy to spot on the street. These innocent vagabonds, who trace their roots to nomadic people from ancient India who migrated to Europe around the fourteenth century, were quickly imprisoned and eagerly killed, primarily because they seemed ungovernable.

Ukrainians. Four to five million Ukrainians lost their lives during World War II. About one million were soldiers who were captured by the Germans and then were killed or died in prison. Able-bodied civilians were shipped westward from their native Soviet Union to Germany and worked in factories or on farms until they fell, exhausted, and died or were killed. The postwar Ukraine seemed almost empty to the few who survived.

Poles. Three million Poles, almost 20 percent of the entire population of Poland, lost their lives in World War II. In fact, Germany overran Poland so quickly at the start of the war that only 20 percent of Polish deaths were attributed to battle. Many Poles were also Jews — Warsaw alone had Europe's largest prewar Jewish population. Jews and non-Jews alike were hauled to Germany in boxcars as the war intensified and the Nazis' need for labor increased.

Belorussians. More than two million Belorussians, or White Russians, one-quarter of the population, died at the hands of the Germans. One-quarter were prisoners of war. Belorussians often failed to reach prison or concentration camps but were instead killed in retaliation for the activities of their guerrilla fighters. For every German who died as a result of guerrilla activity, fifty to one hundred Belorussian villagers were executed in a hail of machine-gun fire or sealed up to die in a burning building.

Chinese. Japanese soldiers killed several million Chinese, most of them civilians. This killing lasted for almost a decade, beginning with the rape of the city of Nanking in 1937 and ending with executions on the eve of Japan's surrender in August 1945. Once WWII ended, Chinese nationalists and communists began to kill each other in a civil war that did not end until 1949.

No one will ever know how many Jehovah's Witnesses, priests and nuns, pacifists, southern Europeans, Filipinos, Malays and other Southeast Asians, Indians, Burmese, and more were mixed in among more despised minorities and killed, worked, or starved to death. Obviously, many, many Japanese also were killed, not only in attacking or defending Pacific islands as soldiers but on the streets of Hiroshima or Nagasaki as civilians.

A Changed America

The U.S. emerged from the war different in some ways and the same in others. Some believe WWII was the fulfillment of the American Dream because wartime production created a huge middle class, there was a rallying sense of "we're all in this together," minorities began organizing to achieve their aims, and women showed they were as capable as men. On the other hand, many Americans continued to discriminate against minorities while claiming to be religious but failing to live their beliefs. Looking out for their own interests first, many Americans promoted rugged individualism when they should have been thinking of the community, and in matters of global politics, they eagerly assumed that the U.S. had become the center of the universe.

The United States spent millions of postwar dollars on foreign aid, much of it on the Marshall Plan. The Marshall Plan, devised by George Marshall, former general of the Army and Harry Truman's secretary of state, helped get the continent of Europe back on its feet economically. And money, together with General MacArthur's light touch in ruling postwar Japan, helped immensely in making Japan a strong ally that would in a matter of years become a wonder of efficiency and development. Many other states, from Yugoslavia to India to the Philippines, which was granted independence from the U.S. in 1946, benefited from free or low-cost Marshall Plan funds.

But it would be naive to think that this money was handed out for purely humanitarian purposes. The fact is that American gifts, loans, foodstuffs, and technical skill bought and kept many friends for the U.S.

While the United States was busy cultivating its postwar friendships abroad, it had work to do at home, too. The most vivid postwar example of activism at home was the revolution in civil rights. In the years following World War II, civil rights activists pushed the courts and federal government to reject the "separate-but-equal" concept among the races that was accepted in many quarters of U.S. society, including the military. The nation lurched reluctantly toward equal opportunity, one person-one vote, fair-housing policies, an end to discrimination in the workplace, and a new attitude toward equality. Even today, not all of these problems are fully solved. Some real-estate brokers still steer Blacks away from certain neighborhoods, and racist attitudes and actions among many Americans seem always to thrive in the "me-first" climate that comes with economic hard times. But the effort to find solutions is an ongoing one, and it owes some of its energy to WWII — a conflict that extracted a terrible price in lives, expense, and disruption, but was not without its dividends.

Liberating prisoners from Oswiecim, the notorious Nazi death camp in Poland best known by its German name – Auschwitz.

Hiroshima Peace Park is an area of unreconstructed buildings in Hiroshima. Each year on August 6, paper lanterns are offered for the souls of the atomic-bomb victims.

1939
Jan. 5: President Franklin D. Roosevelt asks for a greatly increased federal defense budget

Aug. 2: Scientist Albert Einstein, a European Jew who has fled the Nazis, alerts President Roosevelt to the power of the atomic bomb

Aug. 23: Germany and the Soviet Union sign a secret pact agreeing not to confront each other and to attack and divide Poland between them

Sept. 1: Germany launches a *blitzkrieg* (lightning war) against the Poles; the Soviet Union attacks two weeks later

Sept. 5: The United States declares itself neutral in the war in Europe

1940
June 3: The United States approves selling surplus war materials to Great Britain

June 28: The Alien Registration Act is passed; foreigners living in the United States are not permitted to advocate overthrow of the government

Sept. 14: Congress approves the first peacetime military draft

Sept. 26: President Roosevelt prohibits scrap metal sales to Japan

Nov. 5: President Roosevelt defeats Republican Wendell Willkie to win his third term in office

1941
March 11: The Lend-Lease Act provides for $7 billion in military credits to Britain; Lend Lease for the Soviet Union is approved in November

June 14: German and Italian assets in the U.S. are frozen; Japanese assets are frozen on July 25

June 22: Germany launches a massive attack on the Soviet Union

Dec. 7: Japanese military forces attack Pearl Harbor, Hawaii, killing twenty-three hundred people and sinking or damaging nineteen ships

Dec. 8: The United States declares war on Japan; war is declared on Germany and Italy on December 11 following a declaration of war against the U.S. by the two European powers

1942
As many as 120,000 people of Japanese descent, including 75,000 American citizens, are moved away from the West Coast and placed in detention camps

April 18: U.S. Army Air Corps bombers hit Tokyo and other major Japanese cities

May 15: Gasoline rationing goes into effect

June 4-7: The Battle of Midway in the Pacific Ocean is Japan's first military defeat of the war

Aug. 7: U.S. Marines land on the island of Guadalcanal and are unable to expel the Japanese until February 9, 1943

Nov. 8: The United States and Britain invade North Africa

Nov. 18: The draft age is lowered to eighteen as more men are needed

Dec. 2: The first nuclear chain reaction is produced at the University of Chicago

1943
April 1: President Roosevelt freezes wages, salaries, and prices; meat, cheese, and fats join coffee on the list of rationed items that will eventually include everything from shoes to toilet paper.

May 27: War contractors are barred from practicing racial discrimination

Sept. 9: U.S. troops invade Italy

1944
June 6: U.S. and Allied forces invade Europe at Normandy, France

June 22: The G.I. Bill of Rights, providing veterans' benefits, is signed

Oct. 20: U.S. forces land at Leyte in the Philippine Islands

Nov. 7: President Roosevelt wins an unprecedented fourth term in office, beating New York Governor Thomas Dewey

1945
Feb. 3-11: President Roosevelt, Britain's Winston Churchill, and Soviet leader Joseph Stalin meet at Yalta in the U.S.S.R. to decide when the Soviets will enter the war against Japan

Feb. 19: U.S. Marines land on Iwo Jima

April 1: U.S. forces invade Okinawa

April 12: President Roosevelt dies of a cerebral hemorrhage at age sixty-three; Vice President Harry S. Truman becomes president

May 7: Germany surrenders

July 16: The first atomic bomb is exploded at Alamogordo, New Mexico

Aug. 6 and 9: Separate atomic bombs are dropped on the Japanese cities of Hiroshima and Nagasaki

Aug. 15: Japan surrenders

GLOSSARY

anti-Semitism	hatred of or discrimination against Jews or Judaism; the term *Semitic* refers both to the Afro-Asiatic language group that includes Hebrew and Arabic, and to the people who use Semitic languages or belong to Semitic cultures; these people are usually of Caucasian stock and are primarily Jews or Arabs; as a practice, however, anti-Semitism nearly always applies solely to Jews and their religion; Hitler and the Nazis despised Jews whether they were religious or not, and in fact many persecuted Jews weren't necessarily religious
Aryan	according to Nazi belief, a Caucasian, especially of Nordic (northern European) stock; this category excluded Jews, Gypsies, and various Slavic peoples; some Europeans who wrote and studied about race believed the ancient Germans were Aryans, the people who originated in Iran and migrated into northern India, among other places
blitzkrieg	lightning war; the German word is used whenever a nation attacks its neighbor utterly without warning, as Hitler attacked a number of countries, without previous hostilities or declarations of war
code talkers	military personnel recruited from various American Indian groups to relay orders by radio for air strikes and other events, using their native language to create a code that the Japanese would not be able to break; the best-known group of code talkers were members of the Navajo nation
conscientious objector	a person who, on the basis of religion and moral principles, refuses to bear arms or serve in the military
court-martial	a court of military officers appointed by a commander to try people who commit offenses under military law
draft, the	the selection of personnel for service in the military; also known as conscription; criteria for the draft in the United States include being a physically fit male of a minimal age, intelligence, and physical condition
fascism	a system of government that backs a dictator of the extreme right, usually through the merging of business and state interests; often marked by extreme nationalism, racism, and suppression of opposing views through censorship and terror
"final solution"	following mass resettlement, imprisonment, deportation, and other proposed "solutions" to the "Jewish problem" as mapped out by Hitler and the Nazis: the killing of every Jew in Germany or in German-held territory

isolationism	a national policy of remaining aloof from political or military entanglements of other countries
Nazi	an abbreviation of *National Socialist*; a member of the National Socialist German Workers Party, founded in 1919 and brought to power in 1933 under Adolph Hitler; often said of anyone who advocates policies and beliefs characteristic of a right-wing, or fascist, dictatorship, including racism, anti-Semitism, extreme nationalism, and using terror or censorship to suppress those holding opposing views
partisan	in World War II, a member of a group of fighters who attack or harass an enemy within an occupied territory; also known as a guerrilla
socialist	an advocate of socialism, a system of government in which goods are owned and distributed by the whole community and political power is exercised by the whole community
swastika	an ancient, crosslike symbol, seen in India and in the American Southwest; adapted by Nazi Germany as its most visible symbol
USO	abbreviation of *United Service Organization*; a volunteer organization with storefront-type locations in many cities; a place where a soldier can relax, sip a soft drink, read a magazine, or receive advice or directions; most active in time of war
WASPs	abbreviation of *Women's Airforce Service Pilots*; a group of women, numbering about one thousand, who moved planes by air back and forth across the United States during World War II; these civilian women flew inside the country so that men could fly combat missions exclusively

FURTHER READING

Davis, Kenneth C. *Don't Know Much About History*. New York: Avon Books, 1990.

Ferrell, Robert H., ed. *The 20th Century — An Almanac*. New York: World Almanac Publications, 1984.

Gilbert, Martin. *The Second World War*. New York: Henry Holt, 1989.

Hersey, John. *Hiroshima*. New York: Modern Library, 1946.

Kerr, E. Bartlett. *Surrender and Survival*. New York: William Morrow, 1985.

Levin, Nora. *The Holocaust*. New York: Thomas Y. Crowell, 1986.

Parrish, Thomas, ed. *The Simon and Schuster Encyclopedia of World War II*. New York: Simon and Schuster, 1978.

Perrett, Geoffrey. *Days of Sadness, Years of Triumph*. New York: Penguin Books, 1973.

Salmaggi, Cesare, and Alfred Pallavisini. *2194 Days of War*. New York: Mayflower Books, 1977.

Snyder, Louis L. *Encyclopedia of the Third Reich*. New York: McGraw-Hill, 1976.

Speer, Albert. *Inside the Third Reich*. New York: Macmillan, 1970.

Speer, Albert. *Spandau: The Secret Diaries*. New York: Macmillan, 1976.

Syonyi, David. *The Holocaust: An Annotated Bibliography and Resource Guide*. New York: KTAV Publishing House, 1985.

Young, Peter, ed. *The World Almanac of World War II*. New York: World Almanac Company, 1981.

Zinn, Howard. *A People's History of the United States*. New York: Harper Perennial, 1980.